THE SOMERSET
LIGHT INFANTRY
(PRINCE ALBERT'S)
1685–1959

Liz Grant

Somerset Books

First published in Great Britain in 2004

British Library Cataloguing-in-Publication Data
A CIP record for this title is available from the British Library

ISBN 0 86183 491 7

Somerset Books is a partnership between DAA Halsgrove Ltd
and Somerset County Council (Directorate of Culture and Heritage)
www.somerset.gov.uk

SOMERSET BOOKS
Halsgrove House
Lower Moor Way
Tiverton, Devon EX16 6SS
Tel: 01884 243242
Fax: 01884 243325
email: sales@halsgrove.com
website: www.halsgrove.com

Printed and bound by CPI Bath Press, Bath.

CONTENTS

General inspection of the 1st Battalion, Malaya, 1955

King George V inspecting the 2nd Battalion at Aldershot, whilst the 2nd Battalion was part of the Experimental Mechanised Force, April 1932

The Band leaving Buckingham Palace at the end of the 2nd Battalion's tour of duty as Palace Guard, 17 Aug 1936

FOREWORD

THE HISTORY OF THE
SOMERSET LIGHT INFANTRY
(PRINCE ALBERT'S)
1685-1959
by
Major General P.J. Bush OBE – Colonel of The Light Infantry 1977-1982

To the existing histories of the Somerset Light Infantry (P.A.) can now be added this thought-fully compiled and most readable account of the part played by the Regiment in shaping momentous, as well as less dramatic events, in the military history of our country.

Captured here, in graphic form, is the ever-present loyalty to a cause, personal friendships, and above all pride in the County Regimental family; all of which were abundantly apparent through-out the years and in countless locations where the Regiment was called upon to serve.

Through the use of an amply illustrated text flesh is put upon the bones of past achievements, for no matter how faithfully they have been recorded in earlier publications, they are in honesty, occasionally turgid and difficult to absorb other than by the devoted historians among us.

Here, our attention is drawn in a straightforward manner to the devoted service through the years by all ranks. It serves as well to remind us that those characteristics of bravery, leadership and discipline are found equally today in the Light Infantry Regiment.

The profound changes in Regimental life over many years so well reflected in summarised form provides us with a fascinating insight into the life in war and peace of a distinguished County Regiment from its beginnings in 1685. It will I believe be much enjoyed by readers of all ages.

The invaluable contribution made in the last century by the Territorial Army soldier, the wartime conscript and the National Serviceman has happily not been overlooked. Their devotion to the Regiment is an example and lesson to us all.

My congratulations to Miss Liz Grant of the County Record Office, Taunton. From a great many writings, pictures, and photographs she has selected her material with sympathy and under-standing of the central theme of her work.

I extend my thanks also to the members of the Somerset Museum Trustees sub committee consisting of Brigadier A.I.H.Fyfe DL, Mr J.H.F. Mackie and Lieutenant Colonel D. Eliot for their invaluable contribution to this excellent publication. I also acknowledge the considerable help in proof reading received from the following former members of the Regiment: Captain S.W.Jary MC, Major J.D. Majendie, Lieutenant Colonel D.H. McMurtrie, Colonel J.L. Waddy OBE and Lieutenant Colonel R.G. Woodhouse MBE DL.

All the photographs and other sources used in this book form part of the outstanding archives of the Somerset Light Infantry. As part of a project supported by the Heritage Lottery Fund, the collection has been deposited by the Somerset Military Museum Trust in the Somerset Record Office, Taunton, where it has been catalogued and conserved. The archive can be consulted at:

Somerset Record Office
Obridge Road
Taunton
Somerset
TA2 7PU

General enquiries: 01823 278805
Bookings: 01823 337600
E-mail: archives@somerset.gov.uk
The archive catalogue can be viewed online at: www.somerset.gov.uk/archives

An anti-tank detachment with MOBAT, July 1959

CHAPTER 1

ORIGINS

The Somerset Light Infantry (Prince Albert's) traces its origins to the year 1685, when, in the same month that the Duke of Monmouth raised his disastrous rebellion in the West of England, a new Regiment was created by the Earl of Huntingdon.

Though Britain has reputedly had militia units for local defence since the time of Alfred the Great, a regular standing army did not come into existence until the restoration of Charles II in 1660. Before that date the only permanent military formations were the Yeomen of the Guard and the Gentleman Pensioners (now known as the Honourable Corps of Gentlemen-at-Arms), who together formed the sovereign's personal bodyguard. In the event that soldiers were needed to participate in foreign wars or to suppress uprisings at home, the nobles and gentry were required by the king to muster their retainers. Experienced soldiers with overseas experience were often put in charge of the Regiments thus created. By the late Middle Ages, however, the raising of troops by this method was in decline and 'parish soldiers' were introduced, supplied by the towns and parishes in which they lived.

With the outbreak of the Civil War in 1642, the king granted commissions, usually to the nobility and landed gentry, to enable armed Regiments to be recruited.

In 1645 the first national army consisting of full-time soldiers was created. This was Cromwell's New Model Army, formed after the Battle of Edgehill when Cromwell realised that Parliamentarian troops were no match for the Royalists. He decided that for the Parliamentarians to stand a chance of victory, they needed a well-trained, well-equipped and well-disciplined force. He thus returned to his home territory in East Anglia to form such an army from the local squires and farmers. They soon comprised a body of 22,000 men, one-third of whom were cavalry.

A corporal in 1753

At his restoration Charles II supplied arrears of pay to the New Model Army and then disbanded it. By this point the army had been halved in size and had made itself exceedingly unpopular. Parliament resolved never to have a standing army again and told the king that if he wanted soldiers he must fund them himself. Though Charles naturally did not oppose the disbanding of Cromwell's army, his own rule was still insecure and he soon felt the need for loyal troops. On 23 November 1660 he issued a commission for the raising of a Regiment and named it the King's Royal Regiment of Foot Guards. When, in January 1661, it was concluded that this Regiment was insufficient to guard the king, Charles signed a Royal Warrant establishing the first Regular Army.

Thus was the British Army born, though it was to be another twenty-four years before the precursor of The Somerset Light Infantry was created. In 1685 Charles died and fruitless attempts were made to prevent his Catholic brother, James, Duke of York, from succeeding him. James's reign began peacefully enough, but within months two rebellions were raised, one by the Earl of Argyll in Scotland, the second by the Duke of Monmouth in the West of England. Both rebellions aimed to depose James II in favour of the Protestant duke, Charles II's eldest but illegitimate son. The inadequacy of the militia in suppressing these rebellions provided the king with a powerful argument for increasing the standing army, and soon 12 additional regiments of cavalry and infantry had been formed.

One of the loyal noblemen who now came forward to support the king was Theophilus, Earl of Huntingdon, who was appointed Colonel of one of James's new regiments on 20 June 1685. The earl raised his Regiment throughout the southern counties and located its headquarters at Buckingham. Known as the Earl of Huntingdon's Regiment, it later became the 13th Regiment of Foot and later still, the Somerset Light Infantry.

At its conception in 1685 the Regiment consisted of ten companies of around 60 men each. Privates earned eight pence per day, and the company commanders eight shillings. The uniforms consisted of round hats with broad brims turned up at one side and ornamented with yellow ribbons, scarlet coats lined with yellow, yellow breeches and grey stockings. In addition the pikemen wore white sashes at their waists.

The Regiment's first duty was to guard the prisoners captured after the defeat of Monmouth's army at the Battle of Sedgemoor in July 1685. Once the rebellion had been suppressed, James II reviewed the

The Earl of Huntingdon

newly raised regiments at Hounslow Heath, where the soldiers and officers received the king's thanks for remaining loyal and supporting the throne.

By 1688, however, James II's Roman Catholicism was regarded as an increasing threat by the same nobility and gentry who had failed to support Monmouth three years before, and in November they greeted William of Orange enthusiastically when he arrived at Torbay at the beginning of the 'Glorious Revolution'. The Earl of Huntingdon, a Catholic himself, remained loyal to the king, but most of his officers and soldiers supported the Protestant cause. James II fled to France and William of Orange promoted Lieutenant Colonel Ferdinando Hastings, the Protestant cousin of the Earl of Huntingdon, to the Colonelcy of the Regiment, now to be known as Hastings' Regiment of Foot.

The accession of William of Orange and his wife Mary as joint sovereigns did not go unopposed, especially in Scotland. The Highland clans remained loyal to James, and under the leadership of Viscount Dundee fought a Royal Army, including Hastings' Foot, at the Battle of Killiekrankie on 27 July 1689. Though the clans won this brief but bloody encounter, the death of Viscount Dundee in the charge at Killiekrankie effectively brought the Jacobite cause in Scotland to an end. Hastings' Foot distinguished itself for steadiness and bravery at Killiekrankie, despite the outcome of the battle, and the following year formed part of the Royal Army, led by William III, which defeated James II at the Battle of the Boyne in Ireland. James's support had remained strong in Catholic Ireland, but now he fled to permanent exile in France and the Glorious Revolution was at last secure.

Three months after the Boyne, under the command of the Duke of Marlborough, Hastings' Foot took part in the capture of Cork and Kinsale, spending the next year on garrison duty and in countering local resistance from Irish Catholics. In 1692 the Regiment formed part of a force sent to France to discourage French expansion in Europe. It did not remain in Europe long and wintered back in England, where it remained for the rest of the war. In July 1693 the Regiment sent a draft of 150 men to Flanders to fill the losses after the Battle of Landen. In 1695 Colonel Hastings was accused of over-charging his soldiers for articles he was meant to provide, along with accepting bribes for promoting less-deserving officers in his Regiment. Having been proved guilty of extortion, Colonel Hastings was deprived of his commission, which on 24 March 1695 was conferred on Lieutenant Colonel Sir John Jacob.

In 1700, with the French possession of the Spanish Netherlands and the imprisonment of the Dutch garrisons stationed in the border towns, 12 British battalions, including Jacob's Foot, were sent to Holland, arriving in July 1701. Whilst there the Regiment saw a change in Colonel again, to James, Earl of Barrymore. Under the Earl of Marlborough, the Regiment took part in 1702 in the sieges of Venloo, Reuremonde and the Fort of Chartreuse.

Following the death of King Charles II of Spain in 1700, the English had concluded a treaty with Portugal in support of the Hapsburg Archduke Charles's claim to the Spanish throne, against Philip, Duke of Anjou who was supported by Spain and France. Barrymore's Foot was selected to go to Portugal, where it arrived in March 1704, before being sent to Gibraltar to protect it from a combined French and Spanish invasion, remaining there throughout the siege. It was during this siege that the Regiment received its first battle honour. In the early months of 1705 the Franco-Spanish forces fired a total of 8000 bombs and 70,000 round shot at the fortress, and in February almost succeeded in an attack on the Round Tower. This failed thanks to Lieutenant-Colonel Montcal and 500 men of the Regiment who counter-attacked fiercely. After a month of heavy rain, the besiegers gave up and left.

The Regiment was relieved from garrison duty and joined the Earl of Peterborough's expeditionary force to Spain, where they took part in the capture of Barcelona and of San Mateo. In 1706 the Earl of Peterborough summoned the Regiment to Vinaros in Spain where he was in need of a cavalry regiment to help in an attack on Valencia. He managed to find 500 Spanish horses to form a cavalry unit and, having been pleased with the actions of Barrymore's Foot, he decided to turn it into a regiment of dragoons. The soldiers discovered this as they approached Oropeso where they were met and reviewed by the earl who presented them with the horses and constituted them as a corps of dragoons, under Colonel Edward Pearce. Thus Barrymore's Foot became Pearce's Dragoons, whilst the Earl of Barrymore with five of his officers and 20 non-commissioned officers returned to England to raise a new regiment of foot, which was accomplished in just six months.

Just two years later the Regiment returned to Portugal, where, in 1709 it saw its first real defeat, on the banks of the river Caya. In May 1709, the Spanish and French forces, under the Marquis de Bay, marched towards Campo Mayor, whilst the British and Portuguese forces were camped at river Caya. It was decided by the Portuguese generals to

march towards the enemy and attack them, against the advice of the British generals. However, as soon as the enemy's cavalry began to charge, the Portuguese cavalry fled the field of battle leaving behind its cannon. With Barrymore's Regiment leading the infantry, they managed to push back the Franco-Spanish cavalry and recapture the lost guns. The Portuguese cavalry failed to return to support the infantry and it soon found itself surrounded by a numerically superior force. Barrymore himself, along with four captains, eight lieutenants, eight ensigns, three volunteers and up to 300 non-commissioned officers and men of the Regiment, were taken prisoner by the Franco-Spanish army. They remained as such for a year until they were exchanged for a group of French prisoners who had been captured by Marlborough in Holland.

The Regiment then returned to Gibraltar where it remained on garrison duty for the next seventeen years.

Whilst in Gibraltar Barrymore gave up the colonelcy to Colonel Stanhope Cotton, who also became Lieutenant Governor of Gibraltar. In 1725 Colonel Cotton died and the colonelcy was conferred on Brigadier General Lord Mark Kerr. The Regiment was successful in repulsing a second Spanish attack in 1727, returning to England in 1728. The Regiment saw another change in leadership in 1732 when Lord Mark Kerr was replaced by Colonel John Middleton. He died in 1739 and was replaced by Colonel Henry Pulteney.

It was as Pulteney's Regiment of Foot that the Regiment saw action in the War of Austrian Succession. When, in autumn 1740 Charles VI, the Holy Roman Emperor died, the question of his succession arose. Thus with the prospect of war, in 1742 Pulteney's Regiment was sent to Flanders under the Earl of Stair, to support the claim of Emperor Charles's daughter, Maria Theresa, to the Austrian lands. In March 1743 war was declared against France and the British and Austrian forces began to march against France's ally Prussia. On 27 June the British troops marched for Hanau, whilst a group of French forces crossed the River Maine and formed up for battle near the village of Dettingen in Germany. The British infantry, of which the Regiment was part, shattered the French troops, leading to a decisive British victory and the addition of Dettingen to the Regimental Colours. The Regiment again saw action two years later at the Battle of Fontenoy, where Pulteney's Regiment lost nearly 100 officers and men. The outcome was a victory for the French, but at great cost.

The Jacobite Rebellion of Bonnie Prince Charlie in Scotland in 1745 resulted in the Regiment being recalled from Flanders to join the English forces sent to oppose him. They took part in the Relief of Stirling Castle, which was being held by the Jacobite prince, then marched towards Falkirk. Here they arrived and camped on 16 January 1746, later fighting at the Battle of Falkirk Moor. After the raising of the Siege of Stirling, the Regiment joined in the pursuit of the Jacobite army, which withdrew towards Inverness. On 16 April the Jacobites were discovered on Culloden Moor and the English drew up into battle formation. Pulteney's Regiment was originally part of the reserve, but was soon ordered up and placed on the right of the line. The English forces secured total victory and Bonnie Prince Charlie fled to France. Tradition has it that owing to the good conduct of the Regiment during the Battle of Culloden, the Duke of Cumberland, as a mark of distinction, declared that the sash worn by senior non-commissioned officers (SNCOs) should be worn over the left shoulder with the knot tied on the right side, whilst the rest of the Army continued to wear theirs on the left. This tradition continues in today's Light Infantry, although there are conflicting theories as to its origin.

After the English victory in Scotland the Regiment returned to Flanders, taking part in the Battle of Val against the French in 1747, then returning to Britain in 1749 until 1754, when it was sent to Gibraltar. During the Regiment's sojourn in Britain, a Royal Warrant of 1 July 1751 brought in consistency in uniforms, standards and colours, along with the system of numbering the Regiments of Foot according to their precedence in a complex hierarchy. Thus Pulteney's men became the 13th Regiment of Foot. The 13th remained stationed at Gibraltar for the duration of the Seven Years War, until 1762 when it returned to England. In June 1766 General the Honourable Henry Pulteney resigned and was replaced as Colonel by His Royal Highness William Henry, Duke of Gloucester. In 1767 the Duke of Gloucester was promoted and Major General the Honourable James Murray became Colonel. The following year saw service in Ireland and a move to Minorca was made in March 1769. With the outbreak of the American War of Independence the Regiment returned to England, carrying out garrison duty until November 1780. Now under the command of Brevet Colonel David Ogilvie, it embarked for the Leeward Colonies to increase the British strength there and to ensure that the French West Indies, which had been taken by the British, remained in their hands. With American Independence the Regiment returned to Britain, staying until 1783.

In a letter dated 11 October 1782, George III decreed that all regiments should be linked with a county in order to aid the recruiting of new recruits. At the time, the 13th Regiment was stationed at Frome in Somerset, and was given the title of the 1st Somersetshire Regiment. This was the beginning of the county's association with the Regiment, which continues through its successor, The Light Infantry up to the present day.

In 1783 the 13th Regiment moved to Ireland under the command of Lieutenant Colonel Thomas Coppinger Moyle. Orders were received in 1790 for the 13th to be ready for active foreign service in a direct response to the French Revolution. As the revolutionary ideas spread across the Atlantic to the French Caribbean the British Government felt that its presence there should be reinforced in order to limit the backlash throughout the islands of the British Caribbean. In July 1790 the 13th, under Lieutenant Colonel John Francis Cradock, sailed for the Windward and Leeward Islands, arriving in Barbados in November. By January 1791 the Regiment had been sent as reinforcement to Jamaica and from there, in September 1793, to St Domingo to assist the French planters facing a slave uprising. As it took part in a series of skirmishes and sieges, it was yellow fever that proved to be more deadly than the opposing slave forces, and the Regiment was reduced from 305 men to just 60 by its return to England in August 1795.

The period from 1797 to 1799 was spent in Ireland, where the 13th saw little action owing to its reduced numbers. Having regained full strength it returned to England in March 1800 to prepare once more for foreign service. With the Spanish monarch again joining forces with the French in the war against Britain, the Government decided an attack on Spanish ports was called for. The 13th set sail, under Lieutenant Colonel Lawrence Bradshaw, for the Bay of Corunna on 31 July 1800, and then proceeded to join the British force commanded by General Sir Ralph Abercromby at Cadiz. The force then sailed for Gibraltar. Meanwhile, with French forces under Napoleon occupying Egypt, it was believed by the British Government that Napoleon's aim was India, so the British forces at Gibraltar, including the 13th, were dispatched to relieve Egypt.

The British fleet arrived off the Bay of Aboukir in Egypt on 1 March 1801 but the adverse weather meant it was a week before the forces could attempt to land. Meeting Menou's French forces on the beach, the British managed to push them back, then advance along the narrow peninsula between Lake Madieh and the sea, towards Alexandria, where the Regiment was involved in heavy fighting that took the British forces within 10 miles of the city. Alexandria was surrounded, leaving the path free to Cairo, which surrendered on 27 June. In recognition of the 13th's role in the battle, the Sphinx and Egypt were added to the Regimental Colours, and the officers of the Regiment received the Turkish Medal.

After the peace signed at Amiens on 27 March 1802, the Regiment sailed to Malta, where it remained for a year before returning to Gibraltar. In November 1805 it was relieved from garrison duty at Gibraltar and returned to England, then on to Ireland in 1807. On 26 January 1808 the 13th left for the West Indies once again, arriving at Bermuda on 26 March 1808. An expedition was soon organised to take the island of Martinique from the French, with the Regiment forming part of the land

forces under Lieutenant Colonel John Keane. In a short campaign of only three weeks the French Garrison of Martinique surrendered and the name of the island was added as a battle honour to the 13th's Regimental Colours. About a year later a similar action was carried out in Guadeloupe, with the French forces surrendering after only ten days.

The landing of British troops in Egypt, 1801

In 1813 the Regiment sailed for Halifax in Canada to take part in the war which had developed, as a result of the French Revolution, between the USA and Great Britain. Here on the border between Canada and the US the men were joined by Lieutenant Colonel William Williams, a British officer with a reputation for handling light troops who had made a name for himself during the Peninsular War. The War of 1812 was characterised by small skirmishes and attacks on outposts, with the Americans trying to invade Canada via the Richelieu River; it continued until 1815 when peace was concluded with America. The 13th gained success at Burton Ville, in an action at La Cole Mill, and in putting a garrison of 1200 American militia to flight with hardly a shot fired. With Napoleon's escape from Elba, it was hastily recalled and embarked from Trois Rivières in Canada but could not reach England in time to take part in the Battle of Waterloo.

Britain was now a world power, which brought with it the responsibility of policing that world. The 13th, up until this point, had been involved in building this power; for the next hundred years it would be occupied in maintaining and consolidating the power of the British Empire.

The years from 1817 to 1823 saw home garrison duty in England, Ireland, Jersey and finally Guernsey. Then in 1823 came selection for service in India, before which it was constituted as a corps of Light Infantry from 25 December 1822. The Regiment embarked for India in January 1823 under Lieutenant-Colonel M'Creagh and Major Robert Henry Sale, arriving in Calcutta in May. This was to mark the beginning of a long association with the Indian subcontinent, one that was to last until February 1948 when the 1st Battalion. The Somerset Light Infantry was the last British unit to march out of a newly independent India.

CHAPTER 2

TO THE GATES OF JELLALABAD
1824–1849

FIRST BURMESE WAR, 1824–1826

Burma, lying on the edge of British India, was at first a thorn in the side of the East India Company and later an ideal opportunity for the expansion of its territory. Before 1824 the King of Ava had become increasingly aggressive and expansionist towards his immediate neighbours and British India. In 1766 the Burmese had seized Tenasserim from Siam; 1784 saw the incorporation of Arakan into the kingdom of Ava and 1813 saw the conquering of Manipur, which lay near the Surma Valley. This expansion and advance towards the Indian border made an Anglo-Burmese war inevitable. The British, involved in other areas of India, tried to delay the inevitable. Between 1795 and 1811 a number of peace emissaries were sent to Burma to try to placate the king, but to no avail. In 1816, with the British involved in a conflict with the Pindaris in India, the King of Ava sent a letter to Lord Hastings demanding the surrender of Chittagong, Dacca, Cassimbazar and Murhidabad, all of which lay along the Indian-Burmese border, in what is now present-day Bangladesh. These demands were ignored by the British. From 1821 to 1822 the Burmese conquered Assam and in September 1823 they seized the Shalpuri Island near Chittagong, which was owned by the East India Company. Preparations then followed for a Burmese attack on Bengal. These events pushed the British to the edge and on 24 February 1824 Lord Amherst declared war on Burma.

Whilst tensions had been developing along the Indo-Burmese border the 13th Light Infantry, had been ordered in October 1822 for service in India, setting out in January 1823. Amongst the officers who sailed for India were Robert Sale, who was to lead the Regiment through the first Afghan War, and Henry Havelock, who gained his commission in 1815 in the Rifle Brigade before transferring to the 13th in 1822. Although he had seen no active service Havelock was deeply interested in war yet also highly religious. His role in the Army, especially the part he played

General Sir Henry Havelock

subsequently in the Indian Mutiny of 1857, earned him a reputation as a fearless soldier committed to his Regiment. Having arrived in India, where it was quartered at Fort William, the Regiment heard of the declaration of war against Burma and its orders for involvement.

Previously, all British actions against Burma had been land based, but it was now decided to attempt an amphibious attack to take the town of Rangoon on the river Irrawaddy. A joint naval and infantry expedition was assembled at Port Cornwallis in the Andaman Islands, under the joint command of Brigadier General Archibald Campbell and Commodore Grant. The military force comprised two elements: the first from Bengal, which included the 13th Light Infantry and the second element from Madras. The combined strength of the force was 11,000 men and 42 guns. No land transport was provided and supplies were reduced to a minimum. It was expected that the men of the army should live off the land. The forces were assembled by 2 May 1824, with the 13th under command of Major Robert Sale.

A photograph of a water colour drawing by a Private in the 13th representing Major Sale, saving a soldier and killing a Burmese chief

The first action to involve the 13th was the deployment of three companies, along with a detachment from the 40th Bengal Infantry, to seize and occupy the island of Cheduba on the Arakan coast. The rest of the forces set out for Rangoon and on 10 May anchored within the bar of Rangoon River just 15 miles from the town. Detachments, including the 13th, were landed to cover the disembarkation of the remaining forces. The 13th, under Major Sale, landed at the river gate, meeting no resistance. The attack had been a complete surprise. But during the first night on shore the British and Indian forces, flushed with success, discovered a European brandy store, which they proceeded to enjoy, before looting the neighbouring areas. Half the town was destroyed by fire, with the remaining half being saved only through the swift actions of the sailors from the fleet in the harbour.

On 12 May the remainder of the forces was disembarked. The following fortnight saw the town being placed on a defensive footing. But the Burmese forces were not a walk-over. With up to 50,000 men armed with muskets, swords and spears and well practised in jungle warfare, they soon set to, building barricades and entrenching themselves in the jungle surrounding Rangoon. The weather also played a role, with the monsoon breaking not long after the landing of the British forces. Soon the country was awash and disease was rife.

It was decided by Archibald Campbell that to hold a merely defensive position would endanger the morale of his forces so he ordered an attack on the forces surrounding Rangoon. The going was hard; the artillery had to be manhandled through dense jungle terrain and the Burmese villages were heavily defended. But slowly the Burmese forces were pushed back up the Irrawaddy Valley. In turn the towns of Kemmendyne, Bassein, Prome and Simbike all fell, with Majors Sale, Dennie and Thornhill of the 13th all playing leading roles.

Prome, from the heights occupied by the 13th Light Infantry drawn by Captain Kershaw

By February 1826 the Anglo-Indian forces had advanced 300 miles from Rangoon to the town of Yandaboo. The Burmese capital lay just four days' march away, at the town of Ummerapoora. The advance on the capital began. On 9 February 1826 the 13th led a night attack on the enemy stationed on the open fields near Pagahm Mew, which resulted in them fleeing. The advance was continued to Ummerapoora until on 24

February 1826 the King of Ava sent out a ratified peace treaty to the British and agreed to pay the expenses of the war and to forego a considerable part of his territory. Henry Havelock was amongst the British representatives who advanced to the capital to receive the ratification of the treaty.

The first Burmese War was a brilliantly handled campaign, fought in trying conditions against a large opposing force. Sale, Dennie and Thornhill were awarded the honour of becoming Companions of the Order of the Bath, and Ava was added to the Regiment's battle honours. When in 1851 the General Service Medal was issued for campaigns in India, the bar 'Ava' was added and 15 officers were still alive to receive it. The Burmese campaign also helped to build the celebrity status of Sale and the other officers and started the Regiment on its long links with India and its reputation for courage.

The First Links with India, 1822–1838

Though India was always known as the jewel in the crown of the British Empire, it did not come under royal jurisdiction until 1859, after the Indian Mutiny. Before this date the country had been under the control of the East India Company. The British influence in India began during the middle of the eighteenth century, but it took nearly eighty years for the political transition to be complete. Bombay had become a British possession in 1662 and the East India Company had begun trading from there, enjoying steady prosperity from 1709. In the years before 1859 the Army in India belonged to the East India Company and consisted of separate regiments of European and Indian troops led by European officers. From 1709 the East India Company administered India through three presidencies, Bengal, Madras and Bombay, each of which had its own army. These forces were originally recruited by the Company to defend its trading posts but, as its influence spread and trade increased, the armies began to develop into full battalions, taking on a more developed military role. In 1748 the three armies from the separate presidencies were put under the central control of Major Stinger Lawrence.

Just nine years later Robert Clive began to organise, equip and train the Indian Army along the lines of the British Army. It was at this time that all battalions were led by European officers. In addition to the Army of the East India Company, there were regiments and battalions of the regular British Army which were sent firstly to aid the Company in times of crises, later becoming permanently stationed in the country and conducting tours of duty.

The Somerset Light Infantry was first sent to India in 1823. Of the next thirty-six years, thirteen were spent in India, whilst from 1858 until the end of the Second World War one or other of its two regular battalions was normally stationed in India. The long relationship that developed between the Regiment and India was one based not on conflict but upon garrison and colonial duties. The Regiment's first arrival in 1823 was just a stopover on the way to the first Burmese War. Its first stay of any length was between 1826 and 1838; returning from service in Burma the Regiment reached Calcutta in mid-April. This first service in India was typical of most that followed, entailing moving between forts and stations where the men spent a few months before moving on. After the First Afghan War the Regiment was to return to India where it would be greeted with great honours. Again time was spent moving from one station to the next, rebuilding defences and being re-equipped. Occasionally such routine activities were interspersed with suppressing local uprisings and hostilities; one such event occurred in June 1844 when the Regiment put down a mutiny of the 64th Bengal Native Infantry.

THE FIRST AFGHAN WAR, 1839–1842

Afghanistan's rise to world fame in 2001 is not without precedent. For a hundred years the country was a thorn in the side of the British Empire, erupting into conflict on three separate occasions: firstly in 1839 during which war the Regiment won its greatest battle honour and the praise of Queen Victoria, secondly in 1878 and for the third time in 1919, which again saw the involvement of the Regiment. Afghanistan provided a buffer state between the British interests in India and the expansionist policies of the Russian Empire. It was therefore in the British interest to, at least, keep the rule of Afghanistan neutral, but if possible to install a pro-British leadership. It was this fear of Russian expansion and the wish to ensure a pro-British rule, which led to a century of conflict.

The first problems with Afghanistan began in 1837. A Persian army, with the encouragement and backing of Tsarist Russia, invaded western Afghanistan and besieged the city of Herat. The British Government, seeing this as a direct threat to its interests in India, began to fear an invasion of the north-west of Afghanistan by Russia. Added to this, Shah Shoojah, a former monarch of Afghanistan, had been overthrown and exiled to India, and Runjeet Singh, the Sikh leader and a firm ally of the British, had been attacked by the dominant Afghan chief Dost Mahomed Khan. These factors led to a tripartite treaty between the British, Runjeet Singh and Shah Shoojah, which aimed to restore Shah Shoojah

Amir Dost Mahomed Khan

as the ruler of Afghanistan, thus making his country pro-British and halting Russia's imperialist activities.

The plan was deeply flawed from the beginning. Shah Shoojah was seen by the Afghan people as unlucky and was despised by them; this would mean that he could be kept in power only by a constant supply of British arms and force. Shah Shoojah's regime was also to be backed by Runjeet Singh and his Sikhs, who were the bitterest enemies of the Afghans. This fact alone would mean that any invasion of Afghanistan would be sorely opposed, but linked with the hostility towards Shah Shoojah the expedition was sure to fail. Britain and her allies overlooked these factors and an Anglo-Indian force, titled the Army of the Indus, was assembled.

The Army of the Indus consisted of one brigade of artillery, one brigade of cavalry and five brigades of infantry, these troops being in two divisions, one commanded by Sir Willoughby Cotton, the other by Major-

The Durbar-Khaneh of Shah Shoojah, Kabul

General A. Duncan. In addition to this force a Bombay contingent was raised and proceeded to Karachi, while Shah Shoojah raised a further 6000 Indian soldiers. The 13th Light Infantry had been selected to form part of the infantry brigades and arrived at Ferozepore in India on 26 November 1838. It was whilst the Army of the Indus was forming at Ferozepore, that news was received of the lifting of the Persian Siege of Herat. The expedition was not called off, but the army, on the order of the Commander-in-Chief, General Sir Henry Fane, was reduced in size, with the participating brigades being drawn by lots.

It was decided against advancing into Afghanistan through the Khyber Pass, renowned as a dangerous passage. Instead the Army of the Indus marched across Baluchistan to pass through the Bolan Pass, with the objective of Kandahar. This decision almost ended the expedition before it started. Baluchistan could barely feed its own inhabitants, let alone a marching army of some 30,000 troops and camp followers, and in the first month over 10,000 of the army's camels died from a lack of forage, whilst the troops were put on half rations and the camp followers on quarter rations. Stragglers were soon picked off by the local hostile tribes.

At this time the 13th Light Infantry, as part of the 1st Bengal Brigade of the Army of the Indus, was under the command of Colonel Robert Sale, who was to become a military icon and a Victorian celebrity. Sale started his military career at the age of fourteen as an ensign with the 36th (Herefordshire) Regiment of Foot, then served through five campaigns with the 12th (East Suffolk) Regiment of Foot including the capture of

Major General Sir Robert Sale

The entrance to the Bolan Pass from Dadur

Mauritius in 1810. He joined the 13th (1st Somersetshire) Regiment of Foot in 1821 at the age of forty, gaining his reputation for fearlessness during the first Burmese War of 1824. Nicknamed 'Fighting Bob', Sale was a leader who inspired true devotion in his men, especially during the first Afghan war, after which he received the Knight Grand Cross of the Order of Bath and the thanks of Parliament.

In April of 1839 the Army of the Indus reached Kandahar. On the approach of the British Army the rulers of Western Afghanistan had fled, some surrendering, others waiting for a better opportunity to attack the invaders, thus leaving the passage into Kandahar unopposed. The town provided the badly needed supplies and provisions for the Army, along with a chance for recuperation after the 1000-mile march from India. Whilst the Army was stationed at Kandahar, Colonel Sale and a contingent of troops set out against the fort of Girishk, taking it and occupying it with little opposition before rejoining the rest of their men. Even here, their first base, the troops were beset with problems such as fever, dysentery and jaundice.

Towards the end of June 1839 the Army, minus a small garrison, set out for Kabul. Along the route stood the fortress of Ghuznee, but the siege guns having been left at Kandahar, it was proposed to storm the fortress without them. All the gates, bar one, had been bricked up and so it was decided to attempt to destroy the only unreinforced gate in order to gain access to the fort. At dawn on 22 July 1839 an explosion blew the gate free and a storming party of the 13th, led by Colonel Dennie, rushed in. The rest of the Brigade, led by Sale, soon tried to follow, but confusion reigned as the Afghans tried to leave the fort; hand-to-hand fighting followed, leading to a British victory, at a cost of 17 lives and 165 wounded. With the fall of Ghuznee the road to Kabul lay open. On 6 August 1839 Shah Soojah entered Kabul to an unsettling silence. It appeared to him and the Army of the Indus that the campaign had been a success and its aim of placing Shah Soojah on the throne had been achieved.

The fortress and citadel of Ghuznee and the two minars

The next twelve months saw the continued occupation of Kabul, Kandahar, Ghuznee and Jellalabad. The campaign was deemed so successful that a considerable part of the Army of the Indus was recalled

The city and fortress of Kabul

The Bala Hissar and the city of Kabul

to India, with the 13th chosen to remain. However, Dost Mahomed Khan was still at large. Surprisingly, after a brief skirmish in October 1840 he surrendered to the British authorities in Kabul, from where he was exiled on pension to India. At the same time, Sir Willoughby Cotton, the British Commander in Afghanistan, embarked for India, leaving control of the British forces temporarily in the hands of Sir Robert Sale until the arrival of Cotton's replacement, General William Elphinstone, a veteran of the Peninsular War at whose door the catastrophes of the following year can be laid.

On the face of it the Afghanistan campaign seemed successful: the major towns had been occupied, Shah Soojah had assumed the leadership of the country and Dost Mahomed Khan had been exiled to India. It was decided in February 1841, following the arrival of a brigade under the command of Lieutenant Colonel John Shelton, that the Regiment and some native units could return to India. The summer of 1841 passed peacefully and with the arrival of Shelton's Brigade at Kabul in June it was expected that the Regiment would shortly be leaving for India. But the peaceful atmosphere was just a façade, tensions were beginning to develop. Shah Soojah had not gained in popularity since assuming the

The surrender of Dost Mahomed Khan to Sir William Hay Macnaghten at the entrance of Kabul

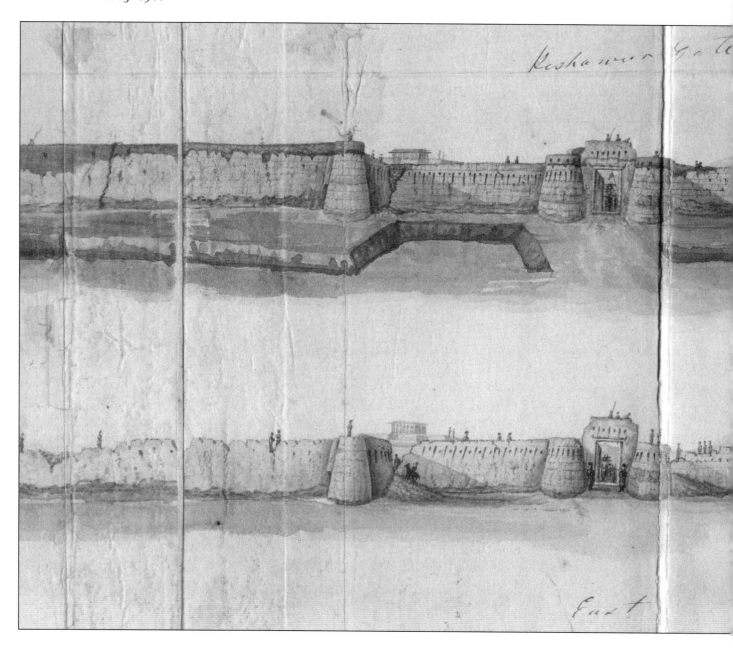

An original sketch of Jellalabad

leadership of the country and only held the position with the help of heavy British backing. All that was needed for hostilities to boil over was a leader to unify the different factions. In October 1841 this leader was found; Akbar Khan, the favourite son of Dost Mahomed Khan, who had been living for the previous two years as an outlaw in Turkestan. At the same time subsidies paid to local Afghan chiefs in order to maintain lines of communication with India were cut. This, linked with growing friction between the British civil and military authorities, led to disturbances in the territory between Kabul and Jellalabad.

Matters came to a head on 9 October 1841 when Lieutenant Colonel Monteith, along with the 35th Native Infantry, proceeded to Bootkhak, which lay just 9 miles from Kabul at the entrance of the

Khoord Kabul Pass. On the night of the 10th they were attacked and suffered heavy losses. In response Sale, along with the 13th Light Infantry, which was 800 men strong, four companies of sappers and miners and a group of cavalry, was sent to join the forces at the Khoord Kabul Pass. On the 12th Sale tried to force the Pass, meeting strong opposition from the Afghan forces who were able to conceal themselves in the rocky terrain. General Sale was severely wounded in the ankle. Colonel Dennie took charge and cleared the heights that controlled the Pass. Sale's force, constantly harassed by the Afghan rebels, with Sale himself on a litter, and with little food, on Elphinstone's orders fought on to Gandamak, a cantonment lying 25 miles south-west of Jellalabad, which was garrisoned by Shah Shoojah's troops.

It was whilst stationed at Gandamak that Sale received news of an Afghan insurrection in Kabul and the death of Sir Alexander Burnes, the assistant to the British Envoy to Afghanistan, Sir William Hay Macnaghten. The latter ordered Sale's force to return to Kabul as long as arrangements for the sick could be made. At the time there were 300 sick and injured, not enough pack animals nor ammunition, and the certain knowledge that the journey to Kabul would have to be fiercely fought every step of the way. In addition Kabul was heavily defended already with sufficient forces to be able to stamp out the insurrection or at worst hold out against a siege until relief forces could be summoned. After consultation with his officers, Sale decided he could not obey Macnaghten's order, and he decided instead to retire to Jellalabad. Sale explains the reasoning for his decision in a dispatch to Governor General T.H. Maddock in India:

> *My retracing my steps on that city was, in a military sense, impracticable, since the first inevitable sacrifice would have been of the lives of 300 sick and wounded, whom I could not have left in depot with the treasonable irregulars at Gundamuck [sic], whilst my cattle was unequal to the transport of my camp equipage, and my ammunition insufficient for protracted operations. In the position which I occupied I could not absolutely command a day's provision or even water, and should have been hemmed in on every side by hostile tribes, amounting to 30 or 40 thousand men.*

The move to Jellalabad was proposed for mid-November, but on the 10th most of the camel and pony drivers deserted, so it was decided to leave the camp equipment and officers' baggage at Gandamak. At noon on 12 November Sale's forces left for Jellalabad but were attacked on the way being saved only by a strong rearguard action by Colonel Dennie. Upon reaching Jellalabad later that night, Sale discovered the walls in ruins, the cantonments burning and the inhabitants fled.

The garrison at Jellalabad comprised 700 men from the 13th Light Infantry, 750 of the 35th Native Infantry, 150 sappers, a handful of cavalry and irregular troops and 14 miscellaneous pieces of artillery. The troops had only 120 rounds for their aged flint muskets and rations for only two days. As they entered the town 6000 Afghans attacked them. In a quick defence 700 of Sale's men, under Lieutenant Colonel Monteith, sallied out from the ruins and put to flight the Afghan force in a battle that was to be named The Battle of Piper's Hill. After this the enemy kept at a safe distance, any spare soldiers were put to rebuilding the garrison walls and a month's rations were requisitioned from the local villages.

The water gate at Jellalabad

The scene of the last massacre at Gandamak, where the European force was destroyed, taken during the 1950s

In the early weeks at Jellalabad, news was received from Kabul that Macnaghten had been lured out of the British lines and murdered; Elphinstone was at odds with his staff and could not make a decision on any action and the Kabul garrison troops were deeply demoralised. At the beginning of January 1842 they learned of the humiliating capitulation of the Kabul forces, which was little more than an unconditional surrender. The British and Indian forces along with their camp followers, 16,500 persons in all, were told that they would be allowed safe passage from Afghanistan. But the Afghans were not above treachery, indeed they were renowned for it and they began to move into position along the withdrawal route of the Army of the Indus. Of this force only one European, Dr Brydon survived. He managed to reach Jellalabad alive; 100 captives, including women and children, including Lady Sale, were taken prisoner and the rest were slaughtered. Dr Brydon's entrance into Jellalabad is recorded in the diary of Lieutenant General Granville Chetwynd Stapylton, at the time a Lieutenant in the 13th Light Infantry stationed at Jellalabad:

'The Remnants of an Army' by Lady Butler, depicting Dr Brydon's arrival at Jellalabad. (It can be viewed at the Somerset Military Museum, Taunton Castle.)

Reproduced by kind
permission of the Tate Gallery

On 13th January our worst anticipations were realised, the troops were all outside digging the ditch round the fort when a European was observed moving towards the Cabul Gate [sic] on a miserable pony. This proved to be Dr Brydon, who, though wounded in several places, alone of the whole Cabul force succeeded in reaching Jellalabad. The account he gave of the situation of the remains of the force after passing the barrier at Jugdulluck when he quitted them, left us but slight hopes that any would reach Jellalabad in safety.

On that night, however, a large lantern was suspended over the Cabul Gate during the night, and the colours of the Regiment by day. Our bugles sounded the advance every half hour during the night for the ensuing week to attract the attention of any who might have escaped, and feared to approach the fort not knowing if it was occupied by friends or foes. All, however, was without success.

The situation was ominous. Kabul had fallen and hostile forces surrounded all the other major garrisons, Kandahar, Ghuzni and Charekar, added to which communication with India was irregular and unreliable. Worse still, Akbar Khan was now free to turn his attentions towards Jellalabad. The garrison, sheltering behind rebuilt and reinforced walls, was fairly confident, having received news on 13 February that a relief force, under General Pollock, was on its way from Peshawar. But just six days later a violent earthquake hit Jellalabad, causing much of the new wall to collapse and for a third of the town to be reduced to rubble. Yet again the soldiers were set to rebuilding the defences, which were sound once more before Akbar Khan's arrival at the end of the month.

The Afghan forces camped just 2 miles away from the town. Afghan siege parties continually attacked the walls but were driven off by sallies from the garrison. In one particularly successful sortie on 1st April 1842 the 13th and 35th Native Infantry managed to round up 500 sheep and goats to bolster their dwindling rations. At the beginning of April a rumour reached Jellalabad that Pollock's relief forces had been destroyed in the Khyber Pass. The situation was indeed bleak; Sale called a Council of War. After much deliberation it was decided to risk everything on a pitched battle with the Afghan force on 7 April 1842, a day that has been celebrated as Jellalabad Day ever since.

Lieutenant Chetwynd Stapylton describes the actions of that day in his diary:

7th April. Daybreak the next morning found the troops drawn up in order at the different gates waiting for the word. Sally was made in three columns with a battery of six nine-pounders between the centre and left columns.

The 13th Light Infantry which formed the centre was rather annoyed by the flanking fire of a small fort not very far from the walls, and though contrary to the original plan by which all these forts were to be avoided,

The original defences of Jellalabad, showing the original state of the walls and the defences built by the 13th

One side of the interior of the square of the Zenana where the British prisoners resided

General Sale ordered the Regiment to bring up their left shoulders and go at it, as there was apparently a breach. Through this breach which was built up with a wall about 7 feet high, the head of our column passed, but found that we were only in an outer part of the fort, and were exposed to a murderous fire from the inner fort and were obliged to pass out on the other side. It was at this fort that Colonel Dennie and some of our best men met their death. The Artillery opened a fire upon the fort to make a breach, but finding that no impression was made, and that the other columns were advancing, orders were given to move on.

Had it not been for this delay, we should have pressed the enemy much more severely, as they would have been unprepared. As it was, we found them all drawn out to receive us. The right column under Captain Havelock 13th, had gone on by the bank of the river to turn the enemy's flank, and were twice closely pressed by the Cavalry, and obliged to form a square. The two other columns moved steadily on with the Artillery in the centre, which kept up so tremendous a fire upon their cavalry that they were forced to retire before us. They were driven right through their camp where they attempted to make a stand, and fired a few shots before deserting their guns.

Just nine days later Pollock's forces arrived at Jellalabad to be met by the Band of the 13th, who played them into the tune of the old Jacobite air, 'Oh! but ye've been lang o'coming'. In the autumn of 1842 the remaining garrisons of the Army of the Indus met in Kabul. On their way there Sale's forces inflicted several more blows to the Afghan forces. Akbar's prisoners were rescued and the bazaar at the centre of Kabul was demolished in revenge for the murder of Macnaghten. The occupation of Afghanistan was, however, short-lived; on 12 October 1842 the forces left for India.

A bazaar in Kabul

The repercussions for the Regiment from the first Afghan War were vast. The Regiment was given the honourable title the 'Illustrious Garrison' by the Governor General and a 21-gun salute was fired at every principal army station that was passed through on its return through India. In England, the Prime Minister, Sir Robert Peel, sang the Regiment's praises in the House of Commons, and Queen Victoria retitled it the 13th or Prince Albert's Regiment of Light Infantry, and changed the uniform facings from yellow to royal blue. A special campaign medal was struck to be awarded to those who took part in the siege. The name Jellalabad was added in a scroll at the top of the regimental crest, together with a mural crown representing the fortress walls of Jellalabad and the initials P.A. standing for Prince Albert's. Three more battle honours were also added to the Regimental Colours: Ghuznee 1839, Afghanistan 1839 and Cabool 1842. For most of the British Regiments involved in the first Afghan War, it was a high point in their Regiment's history. For the 13th Light Infantry, however, it proved to be a glorious campaign – though a costly one.

Chapter 3

A Tale of the Crimea,
Indian Mutiny and Zulu Warriors

The Crimean War, 1854–55

In 1854 Britain and France allied with Turkey to resist Russian attempts to dismember the latter country. At the time the Regiment was in Gibraltar with Lord Mark Kerr as its Colonel. Despite this officer's best endeavours it was not until 1855 that the Regiment was sent to the Crimean War, arriving only in time to take part in the final stages of the seige of Sevastopol. Nevertheless, despite this limited involvement, it was awarded its eighth Battle Honour 'Sevastopol' in regognition of its achievements.

The Indian Mutiny, 1857

Prior to the outbreak of the Indian Mutiny the Regiment was stationed at Port Elizabeth in South Africa, as the British Government believed that a war there was imminent. The Regiment was still under the command of Lord Mark Kerr, a General who had an overwhelming contempt for rank and a rather outspoken manner. These personality traits did not endear him to his superiors and would prove to have a detrimental effect on the Regiment.

Lord Mark Kerr, c.1870s

Although the Indian Mutiny broke out in May 1857 neither the news of it nor the call for reinforcements reached South Africa until August and so the Regiment did not sail for Calcutta until the end of the month. Increasingly, the British Crown had been taking an interest in India and had started to usurp power from the East India Company. By 1834 the Crown was ruler of India in all but name and the final blow came with the Indian Mutiny of 1857. This had its roots in the opposition of the Indian princes to the East India Company, but incorporated dissent against confiscation of property, Western encroachment into Indian traditions and conflict between the Muslim and Hindu communities. The final spark was the sending of Indian soldiers overseas, which was considered to encroach upon caste feelings; in addition the grease smeared on the cartridges of the new Enfield rifle was said to be the fat of cows and pigs, which outraged the Muslims and Hindus.

The orders for reinforcements received by the Commander-in-Chief and Governor-General in South Africa were vague and did not ask for a specific number. It was therefore up to these two men to decide which battalions out of a choice of 10,000 men would be sent. Upon hearing the news Lord Mark Kerr began to press the name of his Regiment, keen to add further glory and battle honours to the growing list already held by the Regiment. At first his requests were denied but after further argument it was agreed that 737 men of the Regiment would be sent in two contingents. The situation that greeted the first contingent's arrival in Calcutta was bleak. Although Delhi had been recaptured, a siege at Lucknow was still in progress, in which Havelock of Afghan and Burmese fame was trapped. Most of Bengal and Oudh was in an unstable state and the lines of communication between the British posts were disrupted and unreliable.

The British forces in India were under command of the Commander-in-Chief, Sir Colin Campbell, who was based at Calcutta overseeing the arrival of reinforcements for the relief of Lucknow. It had been Campbell's intention to appoint Lord Mark Kerr as commander of a column sent to disarm the mutineers of the 32nd Native Infantry Regiment in the Raneegunge district. The regimental history then states that when meeting with Campbell, Kerr remarked that his Regiment had not yet been provided with spare soles nor heels for their boots; this comment led to Kerr being passed over as commander of the column in favour of Colonel Barker of the Royal Artillery. Worse was to follow.

On 15 September the Headquarters Wing of the Regiment was entraining for service in Raniganj. Lord Canning, the Governor-General of India, and Campbell came to see them off, the latter greeting Kerr with a smile which he ignored and then proceeded to answer all Campbell's questions bluntly with just a yes or no. The following day Barker arrived to take control and on 26 October the column commenced its march to the North West Provinces. Two days later two companies of the Regiment were sent under Captain H.M. Jones in pursuit of a group of mutinous sepoys of the 32nd. This left Kerr with three companies, which was barely enough to provide an escort for the artillery. At the end of the day, Sir Colin Campbell and his staff overtook the column and Lord Mark Kerr was summoned. When asked how his regiment was doing Kerr replied, 'I cannot tell how it is, for I see very little of it ... I've got no wing here, only an escort for artillery.' Campbell then tried to explain the choice of Barker over Kerr; he stated that Barker had been chosen owing to seniority of rank, but Kerr argued that Barker had only been a Captain in the same camp during the Crimean War whilst Kerr had commanded a regiment and that Campbell had promised the command of the column to Kerr at Calcutta. The two officers parted company and it became the general belief amongst the officers and men of the Regiment that they lost their chance to help in the relief of Lucknow, the most important and famous battle of the Indian Mutiny, because of Kerr's bad-tempered and rude behaviour.

At the end of November Barker's column, containing the Regiment, reached Allahabad and remained stationed there whilst Sir Colin Campbell relieved Lucknow and moved on to Cawnpore to subdue fighting there. The Regiment spent the next two months moving between Allahabad and Cawnpore, often providing an escort for wounded men or officers' ladies. At the beginning of February Lord Mark Kerr had another meeting with Sir Colin Campbell, at which Kerr forcefully demanded that the Regiment to be sent to the front. Unsurprisingly, this had little effect on the Commander-in-Chief.

Meanwhile, the second contingent of the Regiment, comprising 252 men and nine officers under the command of Major Cox, arrived at Calcutta on 18 and 19 January 1858. Immediately on disembarkation, this contingent marched for Benares and then on to Azimghur, where a small column was formed. Various small parties of rebels had been spotted in the area so tours of the district were carried out before the troops marched towards Gorakhpur, further to the north. With their final defeat at Lucknow the rebels had dispersed into the surrounding countryside. Among this group was Koer Singh, a chieftain who held considerable power over the sepoy army. A group of the 37th Regiment was sent out from Azimghur to engage with Koer Singh, but was defeated and had to retreat to Azimghur with the loss of its baggage. The presence of a large rebel force, estimated to be between 4000 and 8000 men, so close to the town of Benares, a large city crucial to the communication links with Calcutta, was a worrying situation.

As soon as news of the situation in Azimghur reached Allahabad, Lord Mark Kerr was asked to prepare his Regiment. On 27 March, it marched for Benares arriving in two detachments on the 29th and 31st of the month. On arrival at Benares, Kerr's plans for glory were again

On voyage to India, drawn by Arthur Bainbridge, 1853

The interior of officers quarters, drawn by Arthur Bainbridge, 1860

A recruiting poster for the
2nd Battalion, 1864

A view of Sebastopol from the heights in front of the 3rd division of the British Army, during the Crimean War

thwarted; Sir E. Lugard had been sent from Lucknow to Azimghur with a strong force, and Sir Colin Campbell ordered Kerr not to engage the enemy until Lugard's arrival. On 5 April Kerr received an urgent request for assistance from Azimghur, but on Campbell's orders and because of a lack of transport, Kerr waited until the next day before marching towards the town. At 6am the column ran into an ambush that Kerr estimated comprised 10,000 men. The enemy had concealed itself in a mango grove and managed to quickly surround the force and cut off the rearguard from the main forces. The baggage drivers fled, the elephants in the baggage train began to run amok and the cart containing the regimental records was set on fire. The situation was grave and Kerr was advised to abandon his baggage train and force his way through to Azimghur. Instead, he started to bombard a set of buildings which the enemy was using for cover. They joined with three skirmishing companies and with a valiant defence by the rearguard section, the enemy was driven off. The drivers of the baggage reappeared and the convoy was able to rejoin the troops. As a result of this action, the Regiment's first Victoria Crosses were awarded to Sergeant William Napier and Private Patrick Carlin for rescuing wounded men under fire. The main outcome of the Mutiny for the rule of India was the abolition of the East India Company and the replacement of the Company's President by a Secretary of State for India. Queen Victoria in due course became Empress of India. In addition, control of the British Army in India and the Indian Army was passed to the Viceroy in Delhi.

Formation of the 2nd Battalion and Depot

Whilst the Regiment was in India a 2nd Battalion was raised at Winchester in January 1858, with Lieutenant Colonel Horne in command. In 1873 the Depot was formed at Taunton.

The Campaign against Sekukini and the Zulu War, 1877–1879

On 5 January 1875 the 1st Battalion disembarked at Table Bay at the Cape of Good Hope, South Africa. It was the beginning of a four-year stay which would see involvement in a colonial war, the award of two battle honours, the award of the Regiment's third Victoria Cross and the last time the Regiment's Colours were carried into battle.

The first years in South Africa passed quietly enough for the 1st Battalion which was occupied in localised duties such as helping to extinguish bush fires and garrison duty. However, in December 1876 Sir

*A battle scene, drawn by Captain
J.M.E. Waddy*

Theophilus Shepstone, the Secretary for Native Affairs, was dispatched
as Her Majesty's Special Commissioner to Pretoria, the capital of
Transvaal, to negotiate with it on the internal policy of that country.
Shepstone had also been granted, under certain conditions, the power
to annex the Transvaal to the British Crown; a contingent of troops,
including the 1st Battalion, was granted to him, with Captain James of
the 13th acting as his Military Secretary. The Battalion, in order to be
nearer any possible action, was sent to Newcastle, which lay just 36 miles
from the Transvaal border. On 11 April 1877 dispatches were received
from Shepstone ordering the Battalion to cross over into the Transvaal,
but because of delays in obtaining transport, it was not until the 17th that
the forces started their march. As the contingent neared the border
town of Coldstream it was met by Mr Whitehead, the Commissioner of
the Wakkerstroom district, who assured them that no opposition would
be met. A course for Pretoria was then set.

Pretoria was reached on 4 May where the troops met a hearty welcome
and on 25 May, a day after Queen Victoria's birthday (the day had been
set as the 24th, but had been too wet), the British flag was flown for the
first time over the Transvaal. The celebrations did not last long. In
December 1877, in a direct response to an increasingly aggressive attitude assumed by King Cetewayo, the King of the Zulus, three companies
from the Battalion under the command of Major Gilbert, with a detachment from the Mounted Infantry, were sent from Pretoria to Utrecht,
where they arrived on 27 December. The next three months were spent
in reinforcing defences and building a fort. In March it was believed
that the tension with the Zulus had subsided and the three companies
from the Battalion returned to Pretoria.

Again, peace was not to last. In early April Sekukini, an important chief
in the North-East Transvaal, under the influence of King Cetewayo,

*Cetewayo, the King of the Zulus during
the Zulu war*

The 13th Light Infantry in camp just after entering the Transvaal

'On Trek' in the Transvaal

began to cause trouble to the local English and Dutch farmers. In response one company was sent to Middelburg, whilst two others were sent to Lydenburg, both arriving toward the end of April. The presence of the troops did little to ease the situation, as they could do nothing to stop the pilfering of cattle and the burning of colonial homesteads. The situation intensified; Sekukini rose up in open revolt and began to make raids against isolated outposts. On 13 August Colonel Rowlands was appointed to the command of the troops in Transvaal. He authorised the relief of the 13th by the 80th Regiment. The 13th was then to take the field against Sekukini.

On 28 August five companies of the 13th marched for the front. Approximately half the Battalion was employed in garrison duty in forts approaching the Lulu Mountains, where Sekukini's stronghold was located, whilst the other half was available for active operations. The plan of attack was to place a large British presence in the forts on the western slopes of the Lulu Mountains, in order to threaten the enemy from that side, whilst the remainder of the force attacked along the eastern slopes, with the aim of destroying Sekukini's stronghold.

On 3 October Colonel Rowlands set out for the attack on the eastern slopes, his forces including two companies from the 13th. After only 4 miles, fighting broke out, in rocky, dry terrain covered in thick bush. The terrain proved more of a deterrent than the enemy and only 8 miles were covered in the first day. The next day was spent the same way and on the night of 4 October the troops went into bivouac at the base of

A caravan taking supplies to the front, the typical mode of transport

almost insurmountable hills. At about 8pm the enemy was sighted creeping down the hillside in large numbers. Defensive positions were assumed, with the 13th taking the front, and the attack was easily repulsed, with little loss of life. The next day proved unfruitful and on 6 October the expedition was called off owing to a lack of water and forage for the animals.

The action was switched to concentrate on the north. The 80th Regiment freed four companies of the 13th from garrison duty in order to allow them to participate in an excursion into the Steelpoort Valley. An attack on 24 October was unsuccessful but the enemy was located at Tolyana Stadt and a further attack was planned for three days later. This action was successful, the enemy position atop a high hill was captured and the enemy was put to flight, with only 11 British casualties.

Whilst Colonel Rowland's forces had been subduing Sekukini, tensions had been growing in Zululand. Rowland suspended operations and withdrew the majority of his forces to the Zulu border.

It is fair to say that the Zulu War was caused by British aggression. Zululand lay along the eastern seaboard of South Africa, just north of modern-day Durban. Just a few years after the emergence of the Zulu nation British adventurers were attracted to it in search of trade and treasure. By 1840 Natal, a British colony, had sprung up on the southern borders of Zululand. Thirty years later the British had begun to conduct a policy of inclusion, hoping to incorporate their own colonies, the Boer republics and the African regions under a common British rule to aid trade and economic development. The strong Zulu nation was perceived as a threat to this ideal, so in December 1878 the British High Commissioner in South Africa, Sir Henry Bartle Frere, picked an argument with King Cetewayo, believing that the Zulus armed with spears and shields would soon fall under a show of British superiority.

In January 1879 the war began; Cetewayo had forces estimated to number around 40,000 men, all of which were extremely mobile. Lieutenant-General Lord Chelmsford was placed in charge of the British forces, which he organised into five separate columns, of which the 1st Battalion formed part of No. 4 column, based at Utrecht. The aim of the campaign was to secure Natal and the Transvaal from invasion. An ultimatum was delivered to Cetewayo which, upon expiry on 11 January 1879, led to the invasion of Zululand by column Nos 1, 3 and 4, the other two columns remaining in defence.

During the first two weeks of the campaign the British Army met with
unmitigated disaster. On 11 January No. 3 column crossed the
Tugela River at Rorke's Drift, and leaving a small garrison there,
continued to Isandhlwana. On 22 January a huge force of Zulus
attacked Isandhlwana, killing 52 officers and 806 other ranks. They
then attacked the garrison at Rorke's Drift, where just 145 men,
including Lieutenant Chard, a Royal Engineer from Somerset, after
ten hours of fierce fighting, drove off the attacking Zulus.
Meanwhile, the other columns had seen little action and had spent
their time marching between outposts. British morale had been
severely dented by the attack on Isandhlwana. Much ammunition
and all the transport and supplies from the 3rd column had been lost
and it was feared that an invasion of British territory would follow.
Luckily the Zulus did not follow up their success and British forces
gained much-needed breathing space.

At the end of January No. 4 column, including the 1st Batallion, moved
to Kambula Hill, which lay, on the slopes of Ngabaka Hawane mountain.
Kambula covered the approaches to Utrecht and as such was both an
important defensive garrison and also a by-station for captured and
surrendered Zulus. It was whilst stationed at Kambula that Major

A Zulu Prince and his second-in-command at Isandhlwana

William Knox Leet who was awarded the Victoria Cross during the action on the Inhlobane Mountain on 28 March 1879. His horse was shot out from under him and he caught a pack horse carrying ammunition boxes, which he cut off with a knife. This horse was also shot from under him. He then managed to get hold of a third, without a bridle, when he saw Lieutenant A.M. Smith of the Frontier Light Horse on foot just about to shoot himself, Leet took the Lieutenant up behind him, and they rode away from advancing Zulus

William Knox Leet of the 1st Battalion was awarded his Victoria Cross. A contingent had left the garrison to provide support for the forces marching towards Etchowe, when on 28 March 1879 a force of 20,000 Zulus was sighted and the British began to withdraw towards Kambula. Major Knox Leet was in command of a battalion of irregulars and during the withdrawal had rescued Lieutenant A.M. Smith from the Zulus by taking him up on the back of his horse to safety.

The 20,000-strong Zulu force continued to Kambula and on the afternoon of 29 March 1879 formed their traditional attack position resembling a bull's head. A hundred mounted men were sent out of the fort to engage the Zulus' right wing to entice them into making a premature attack. The Zulus duly complied and the British forces retired to the fort. When the enemy came within 300 yards of the garrison it was greeted by tremendous firepower. After a day's fighting, the Zulu forces were driven back, with an estimated death toll of 2000 compared to just 18 British. More importantly the Zulus' resolve was seriously dented for the first time.

The 1st Battalion remained encamped at Kambula until early May when it marched to Mumhla Hill and then on to the Umyanyene River, meeting with Lord Chelmsford in early June. From here the men moved on to the Ityotyosi River. On 18 June the column reach Fort Marshall on the Upoko River and on the 27th they reached Entonjaneni Hill which lay just 16 miles from Ulundi, the Zulu headquarters. Whilst here the Zulu king sent out peace envoys, but there was to be no resolution. On 1 July a body of troops advancing towards Ulundi reached the White Umvolosi River, on the far bank of which a large number of Zulus were encountered. The decision was taken to engage them, as a large undefeated army could not be left on the British flank.

On 5 July the British forces crossed the Umvolosi River, and took up a square formation for battle. The infantry formed a hollow rectangle, with the 1st Battalion on the right flank; the guns and Gatlings were placed in pairs at the corners, with the ammunition and tool carts, the bearer company and Natal Pioneers in the centre. The Zulus advanced on the square but the firepower was too strong. They were finally defeated by an attack from the 17th Lancers. The Battle of Ulundi utterly crushed the military strength of Cetewayo, the Zulu warriors returned to their kraals and their king fled. It was the last time that the Regimental Colours, which remained in use until 1962, were carried in battle.

Left: *Bringing in Zulu spies, Kambula camp, drawn by Captain J.M.E. Waddy*

Below: *A Natal pioneer, drawn by Captain J.M.E. Waddy*

Not long after, on 1 August, the services of the 1st Battalion were no longer needed and it embarked for England in the knowledge that it had played a key role in the Battle of Kambula Hill, the turning point in the war, and in the final victory at Ulundi.

In 1882 the Regiment's title was changed to Prince Albert's (Somersetshire Light Infantry).

Above: *An example of the square formation, a similar method would have been used for the attack on the Zulus at the Umvolosi River*

Right: *The 1st Battalion Band, Zululand, 1879*

CHAPTER 4

OF BURMESE KINGS AND INDIAN UPRISINGS

1885–1898

THIRD BURMESE WAR, 1885–1887

Conflict between Britain and Burma broke out for the third time in 1885. The main spark this time had its roots in the previous two conflicts and the continuing border disputes between the two countries. In 1878 King Mindon of Burma died, to be succeeded by Theebaw and his queen Suphayarlat. Theebaw's succession was celebrated by the murder of 80 possible contenders for the throne, to which British protests were ignored. In addition, royal Burmese trading monopolies started to conflict with British agreements for free trade in the country. These growing tensions between the two countries were heightened with the appearance of the French in Mandalay, which indicated to Britain the possibility of French expansion into Burma. A third Anglo-Burmese war became inevitable.

The main aim was to depose King Theebaw, to assimilate the country fully into the British Empire, to gain control of the raw materials in the country and to join up with the French in Indo-China. The initial objective to capture King Theebaw was achieved quickly. Major General Prendergast, the leader of the expedition, with a force of troops from India, crossed the Burmese border on 15 November 1885 and proceeded up the Irrawaddy River. British steamers had been trading along the Irrawaddy River between Rangoon and Mandalay for many years, so the knowledge of this waterway coupled with the dense jungle terrain of the interior of Burma led to the decision to attack the capital by water. Minhla, 40 miles north of Thayetmyo, a British port, was occupied on 17 November and Mandalay met the same fate just eleven days later. The surrender of King Theebaw soon followed. On 1 December 1885 a proclamation was issued declaring the surrender, dethronement and deportation of King Theebaw to India and the annexation of the country for Britain and Queen Victoria.

Queen Suphayarlat and King Theebaw of Burma, c.1885

It was thought that the war was over; its aims had been achieved and the country remained peaceful for a time, as the Burmese believed the British would soon leave. However, as soon as it was realised that they were there to stay, Burmese soldiers, who had returned to their villages, started to form private armies that aimed to expel the British and return Burma to the Burmese. To cope with this new threat the British established small entrenched forts all over the country. The terrain meant that communication was very difficult; the main routes of communication were the rivers, there were few roads and the soldiers often found themselves marching along dry, sandy river beds in single file. The British forces were split up into many small groups, usually consisting of only two officers and around 40 men, a fact that led to the nickname of 'The Subalterns' War'. The enemy too attacked in small parties, using their knowledge of the country and unhindered by baggage and transport. Thus, there were no significant engagements, rather a series of small skirmishes, with the eventual result of the British successfully wearing down the Burmese. It is telling that for the whole campaign casualties for the 2nd Battalion, taking part in its first campaign, totalled 17 men killed and 35 wounded, whilst 150 men died through disease.

The Battalion, commanded by Colonel W. Knox Leet VC, was stationed in Rangoon prior to the conflict and four companies had left Rangoon, under the command of Major Evans, at the end of November 1883 just as King Theebaw was surrendering. They then took part in the small skirmishes that characterised the conflict. Lewis McCausland, a Sergeant of the 1st Battalion, who had been transferred to the 2nd as the war clouds gathered, describes the early days of the conflict in his memoirs:

The Sergeants of the 2nd Battalion, Rangoon, 1884

Before one had really time to look around it was apparent that something unusual was happening outside ordinary regimental routine and I soon discovered that the consensus of opinion was that hostilities with King Theebaw were now certain and further that an Expeditionary Force was in course of formation at Calcutta. Rumours concerning the coming

campaign were daily increasing and then news was received that the Field Force had left Calcutta under the command of General Sir Harry Prendergast, V.C., an Indian Mutiny veteran and a very experienced and gallant Sapper Officer. Four of our Companies were at once placed on war footing for early advance. My mind became rather restless through excitement but luckily every minute seemed occupied ... our battalion Head Quarters were in May 1886, transferred from Rangoon to Mandalay.

With the continued conquest of the Burmese forces it was decided in early 1887 that the British forces in Burma be reduced, with the 2nd Battalion selected to be among the first to leave. By 31 March 1887 the Battalion was concentrated at Mandalay, before embarking for India on 4 April. On embarkation a farewell address was given by General Sir George White, Commander-in-Chief of the Burma Field Force, to the 2nd Battalion thanking the soldiers for their involvement:

Colonel Leet, and Officers, and men of the 13th Light Infantry, I call you forth today not for the purpose of merely seeing you ... but I wish to express to you the high estimation in which you are held, both by the various Commanders-in-Chief and Senior Officers of this District. As I told the Hampshire Regiment when I had a similar parade two days ago, the Burma campaign was not altogether a test of a soldier's fighting capacities, but that you have been harassed with jungle fighting, worn with marching and afflicted with much sickness, all through which you have come with honours that will only increase the lustre of the regimental reputation.

This is not the first chapter in your military chronicle for as you sail down the river you will see today or tomorrow the town of Pagan and as you look out upon the plain you will see the battlefield, where those same colours unfurled before me now, were fought for (possibly by your fathers) years ago.

One Regiment has the proud distinction of calling themselves the 'First in India', I would suggest that this Regiment, (the 13th) having been in the First (and now the Third) Burmese war, should have added to its many distinguished honours 'The First in Burma'.

Again I must specially mention the splendid disciplinary state of the Battalion the value of which was rendered strikingly apparent but a few days ago.

In saying farewell to you all, I wish you a pleasant voyage down the river, that you may like the quarters for which you are bound, and that also when later, you meet your families, or leave the country and go to your homes, you may meet that reception that your distinguished services in this campaign have fully entitled you. Goodbye.

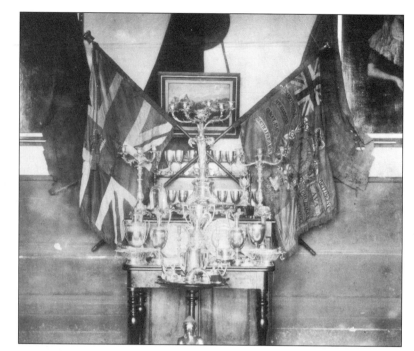

*The 1st Battalion Queen's and
Regimental Colours, c.1889*

The 1st Battalion signallers, Aldershot, c.1890

The 1st Battalion inside Fort Shabkadr, 1897

This first active campaign for the 2nd Battalion, resulted in a British victory and the addition of Burma 1885–87 to the Regimental Colours. In 1888 medals for the campaign were presented to the Battalion. The third Burmese War did not provide the same reputation for the 2nd as had been gained during the first Burmese War, nor did it produce celebrities on a par with Sale and Havelock; however, it was still a successful campaign which achieved its aims, foremost of which was the complete annexation of Burma. Burma remained part of the British Empire until its independence in 1948.

The Mohmand Expedition, India, 1897–1898

The 1st Battalion remained in India until 1864 when it returned to England. The 2nd Battalion paid their first visit to India in 1878, a visit which again saw the soldiers marching from post to post fighting disease rather than foe. In 1893, the 1st returned to India to relieve the 2nd, this time under command of Colonel Henry Hallam Parr. The first two years were spent moving between Lahore, Umballa and Dalhousie. On 29 July 1896, owing to increasing disturbances on the North-West Frontier caused by Mohmand tribesmen, the Battalion received orders to move to Peshawar.

The resulting action, the Mohmand Campaign, was a limited one which saw the Battalion engaged against tribesmen in tropical summer sun along bare stony valleys. The aim of the campaign was to maintain peace along the North-West Frontier and to subdue the tribesmen. On 7 August Brigadier General Elles, who commanded the Peshawar District, received information that a group of Mohmand tribesmen were threatening the village of Shunkargarh which lay under the walls of Fort Shabkadr just 20 miles north of Peshawar. Immediately a small column, which included two companies of the 1st Battalion, was formed to go to the aid of the fort. This column engaged the enemy on 9 August and successfully drove the Mohmand tribesmen back into the hills. The next month was spent marching through the foothills trying to engage the enemy, but again the lack of water and prevalence of disease proved a greater foe. At the end of September, the Battalion was involved in an attack on the Badmanai Pass, in which the enemy put up very little resistance. By the end of the month, the Battalion returned to Peshawar, much weakened by fever and dysentery. Soldiers taking part in the campaign received the India Medal 1895 with the 'Punjab Frontier 1897–98' clasp.

CHAPTER 5

THE LAST COLONIAL WAR AND A TUSSLE IN CHINA
1899–1913

THE BOER WAR, 1899–1902

In 1899 Britain was at the height of her imperial power; her colonial interests stretched from Asia, through India, encompassed South Africa, and her influence was spreading throughout Latin America. Her industrial power was the envy of the world and it seemed that she would remain the largest global power for the foreseeable future. Coupled with this was the 'race for Africa' between the European powers, which strived towards not only colonial expansion but also exploration, Christianisation and material gain. This was the global backdrop to the issues that would culminate in the Boer War.

The factors that were to lead inexorably to the war went back to 1795 when Britain took over the Cape Colony from the Dutch, and British troops started to arrive. At first the Dutch settlers, known as Boers, ignored their new governors and moved away from the administrative centres; they were fiercely independent and refused to accept any outside rule or influence. However, the British authorities began to follow the Boers and hostilities began to develop with the introduction of new laws, such as the order in 1823 for English to be adopted as the official language and the emancipation of British slaves in 1833. This second law struck at the Boers deeply, threatening their economic stability as their farms depended on free labour. It also implied that slaves were now equal, an idea which went against the Boer beliefs that they were the chosen people of God. Unhappy with British rule, a large number of Boers began to move away from Cape Colony. In 1852 the British conceded the Boers self-government and thus the republic of Transvaal was born, with the Orange Free State following two years later. However, the Boers continued to bicker amongst themselves and with the discovery of diamonds in 1867, Britain annexed the Transvaal. Anglo-Boer tensions continued to simmer throughout the second half of the nineteenth century until the Uitlander question became the spark that ignited the Boer War.

Boer prisoners of war pitching tents at Green Point

Boer prisoners of war arriving from the front

The Uitlanders or outlanders were mainly British and during the 1880s the Boers' fears of being swamped by them in local elections led to a build-up of tensions. Coupled with this Cecil Rhodes, the British Prime Minister of the Cape Colony, began to stir up dissent among the British Uitlanders with the aim of incorporating the Boer territories to form one large, strong British South African state. In 1893 the Jameson Raid attempted to invade the Transvaal and incite an Uitlander uprising, but the plan gained little support and it proved a political disaster for the British. At the same time the political base of the Transvaal was strengthened and its people gained support from the German Kaiser, who had his own designs for South Africa. This led to a hardening of British opinion towards the Boers. In 1898 a Boer policeman shot Tom Eggars, an unarmed British miner, but was found not guilty. The verdict enraged the British Uitlanders who sent a petition to Queen Victoria demanding equal political rights in a state where they formed the majority. This led to talks in May 1899 to try to solve the Uitlander problem, but nothing was resolved. Britain was worried that it did not have enough military representation in the area and began to amass troops in South Africa. This brought an ultimatum from the Boers to end troop movements. It was ignored and war was declared.

In October 1899 the British Government issued orders for the mobilisation of an army corps, consisting of three infantry divisions and corps troops, a cavalry division and lines of communication troops. The 2nd Battalion of Prince Albert's (Somersetshire Light Infantry) was selected as part of the communication troops and proceeded to prepare for embarkation. British forces were put under the control of Sir Redvers Buller, Commander-in Chief in South Africa, whose original plan of campaign was to invade the Orange Free State and then advance over the open plains to Bloemfontein. On his arrival the news that greeted Buller was not good; the towns of Mafeking and Kimberley were held by the Boers, in Natal Dundee had been evacuated and Ladysmith was under siege. On 1 November the Boers invaded the Cape Colony. This meant that a large number of the British forces would have to be diverted from the original plan to relieve Ladysmith.

The 2nd Battalion arrived at Cape Town on 20 November and proceeded to De Aar, an important railway junction on the direct line to Kimberley, before new orders were issued for the battalion to move to Durban. By early December the Battalion was moving toward Ladysmith to take part in an attempt to lift the siege, but the military situation swung further against the British and any plans to relieve Ladysmith were postponed. Between the British forces and Ladysmith was the Tugela River, which was bordered by a rocky outcrop of hills, which in turn provided a strong defensive line for the Boers. Buller had to cross this before he could hope to relieve Ladysmith. In January 1900 he was ready to make a second attempt to attack this line.

The attack started well as Dundonald's Mounted Brigade crossed the river and swept northwards. Buller, however, felt that the British needed to seize the hill of Spion Kop in order to maintain his communication lines. The hilltop was seized but the position was perilous; 2000 British troops were squeezed together in a barren area no bigger than a football pitch, which was in open range for the Boer guns. In total 1044 British soldiers were casualties in the defence of Spion Kop, yet it did not fall. In the evening the Somersets, in their first action of the war, were sent to strengthen the defences. Colonel Thorneycroft, meanwhile, who had held control of the hill all day and was unaware of any plans to fight on with reinforcements, ordered an evacuation and the Somersets never reached the top of the hill. Ironically, at the same time the Boers were planning to retire and the British forces were able to retire across the Tugela River in peace.

Early February saw a third attempt on the relief of Ladysmith. The operation lasted a week and was again unsuccessful; the 2nd Battalion covered the British Army's retreat back across the Tugela River. A fourth and final attempt began towards the end of February. Attention was turned to the east where the Tugela, in a great loop, cut the Boer defences. A pontoon bridge was built over the river and the 2nd Battalion had the honour of leading the advance. At 2pm on 21 February the Battalion crossed the river and immediately ran into trouble; its front stretched for about a mile on an open plain totally devoid of cover. About a thousand yards in front of the line lay the lower slopes of Grobelaar's Kloof which was holding the enemy. The Boers were fighting from well-defended positions and soon brought the British attack to a standstill. For four days the British continued to bombard Grobelaar's Kloof, losing 1200 men in the process. Buller then shifted his attentions to the right and began to press the advantage that lay there. In just under twenty-four hours, on 27 February, the Boer line was broken and the road to Ladysmith was open. Ernest Stanton a soldier of the 2nd Battalion describes the initial attack on Grobelaar's Kloof:

The 21st of February my Regiment moved away from their bivouac very early in the morning, not knowing where we were bound for. We knew exactly where the Boers were, having a splendid view of the positions which was only two or three miles away … The Bridge had but all been completed

Groblaar's Kloof, near Colenso, scene of the 2nd Battalion battle during the relief of Ladysmith, taken February 1954

and everything was now ready for the grand old Man's Army to cross the river, going forward bountiful of good hopes, wishing our Army would be successful so as to land us at that beleaguered town where our brothers in arms had been locked up for three months, surrounded by a treacherous enemy full of crafty actions.

My Regiment the Somersetshire Light Infantry was the first to cross and we were passing over the Bridge before the men had time to clear away their tools, and this was about the 6th time that we had crossed the Tugela. Reaching the other side we at once ascended the Kopjes overlooking the river, the trenches and fortifications already being made by our retreating foe … We couldn't see any of the enemy from our position, but the country around about looked very suspicious, and we could still hear the firing of big guns though some distance away. About 1pm we received the order to advance across a large open plain, and try and get to the stony Kopjes some distance in our front. My Company named by the letter 'H' happened to be the advance guard, so we sent out a few scouts well supplied with field glasses, etc, to see if all was clear, a few more men followed some distance after, and then the remainder in one line though in skirmishing order, which means that three or four yards divide every man. Thus, the Regiment was engaged in one way or another, some on the flanks some following in the rear, while some was taking care of our baggage. In a short time you could see the West Country Corps clad in Khaki advancing over a large plain and as we thought to the fields beyond. Whilst skirmishing over the plain, we managed to find several things the Boers had left behind them in their somewhat hasty retreat, the most notable thing of all being a new engine and used by them to enable them to work their search light, the instrument being quite new and to our surprise everything was in perfect order, as you may guess that our people soon took the engine into use … We continued the advance but not for long, as apparently the Boers saw us approaching them, but unfortunately we couldn't see them … suddenly the shots began to come around us and we could see clearly that our position was a dangerous one. The enemy opened a thundering musketry fire, and not only were they firing at us from our front, but we were subject to a crossfire as well, and also practically surrounded. When the firing began we could barely realise our position but it was not a time for considering as we at once got into position and began firing to try and resist if possible the firing of the enemy, the scouts, the firing line and the reserves all forming into one line. Already in possession of one hundred and fifty rounds of ammunition, we began to pour into their position volley after volley wasting no time whatever, but kept up a continuous fire the whole time … The firing got worse and worse and there we were laid out over a great plain and our enemy in the hills around us holding every advantage.

At noon on 1 March 1900 Buller rode into Ladysmith, though the 2nd Battalion had no part in the triumphal march into the city. With the rest of the 10th Brigade they were in the hills north of Colenso, where their attack on the Boers at Grobelaar's Kloof had foundered. After the relief of Ladysmith and the town of Kimberley the nature of the war changed; events finally started to move in favour of the British. Mafeking, Bloemfontein, Johannesburg and Pretoria all came under British control and in July 4000 Boers surrendered in the Orange Free State. It appeared to most, on both sides, that the war was over. However, with the British occupying all the major towns the Boer forces split up and took to the countryside to continually harass the British using guerrilla tactics. The British Army adopted a system of marching and counter-marching, trying to anticipate from where the next attack would come. They also poured in troops, so that by mid-1900 there were over 25,000 British and Imperial troops in South Africa, consisting of regular army, volunteers and for the first time, county militia battalions.

The 2nd Battalion, augmented by one Volunteer Service Company raised from the Regiment's three volunteer battalions, became involved in this constant marching, moving from post to post whilst the 4th (Militia) Battalion was employed as a garrison battalion in East London in the Eastern Cape. The war was one for the horse and the role of infantry tended to be more static and defensive. The Somersets were split between two infantry columns in early 1900 and also supplied two companies of mounted infantry who took part in some encircling attacks in the Transvaal and Orange Free State. The main action the 2nd

Battalion saw, after the successful lifting of the Siege of Ladysmith, was the De Wet hunt. De Wet was a Boer commando-general operating in the Orange Free State, who managed to escape an encircling net ordered by Kitchener, the new commander of the South African forces; this meant that a column of British forces was tied up with trying to track him down. In two months the column marched 560 miles without any sighting of the enemy.

The pattern of the war was days of marching, interspersed with small skirmishes. One such encounter was at Mooifontein in May 1901. Five companies of the Regiment, along with four companies from the Munster Fusiliers, had been entrusted with taking a baggage train, a large number of Boer families, the sick and wounded and livestock, back to Standerton on the Vaal River. On the journey a large body of Boers soon appeared and started to harass the convoy, attacking the rear and the flank. This skirmish lasted six hours and was characteristic of the conditions of the war.

An ambulance bringing a sick prisoner of war into camp

Events carried on in this vein for another year, with both sides trying to wear the other down. In the event the Boers had little hope of standing up to the might of the British Empire and all the resources at its command. In May 1902 peace terms were finally agreed and the British soldiers were congratulated on bringing the war to a successful end. The Somersets won two more battle honours: Relief of Ladysmith and South Africa 1899–1902. They had suffered nearly 200 casualties during the campaign.

CHINA, 1911–1913

Between 1911 and 1913 the 2nd Battalion in China faced a new and different role. It was one that was to become common for all the regiments of the British Army from 1945 but in 1911 was little tested. In 1900 the Boxer Rebellion had broken out in China, with Tsu Hsi, Dowager Empress of the Ch'ing Dynasty, wishing to rid her empire of the foreign influence of Austria, France, Germany, Great Britain, Italy, Japan, and Russia, all of whom staked a claim on China's treaty ports. The rebellion was rapidly crushed by an international relief force that contained soldiers and sailors from eight different countries. Its outcome was that peace keeping was taken over by a combined force from Austria, France, Germany, Japan, Russia, Britain and the United States. The peace-keeping force was stationed along the Tientsin–Peking railway in order to ensure its continued use and to provide a presence to stall any future uprisings.

The 2nd Battalion arrived in China on 23 October 1911 whereupon the headquarters and six companies proceeded to Tientsin, whilst 'C' and 'D' companies made up a Legation Guard at Peking. The situation in China at the time of the 2nd Battalion's arrival was slightly more disturbed than it had been at any time since the quashing of the Boxer Rebellion. This new trouble was not caused by foreign intervention but by rival ambitions between the different Chinese warlords who were continually fighting amongst themselves. British troops in the region were increased, with regiments previously intended for relief being ordered to stay on. In early January 1912 the 2nd Battalion had six detachments positioned along the Tientsin–Peking railway at Fengtai, Lin-Hsi, Leichuang, Kaiping, Wali and Kuyeh.

At first, the 2nd Battalion was employed on garrison duty, the officers spending their leisure time in sporting pursuits such as hunting and fishing, whilst the men beyond guard duty enjoyed social activities. The main purpose of the duty was to provide a protective atmosphere for the British and European residents and merchants living in Tientsin. But on the evening of 29 February 1912 a group of Chinese troops in Peking mutinied, which sparked indiscriminate shooting, looting and burning. The Legation Guard in Peking was continually under arms whilst the city remained in a disturbed state. On 1 March the Chinese 3rd Division, which was quartered in and around Fengtai, also began shooting, and looted the area around the railway. The European women were brought into the fortified post there and in the afternoon were dispatched to Tientsin. On 2 March a further conflict broke out, this

The Officer's Quarters, Tientsin, Dec 1911

Leisure activities, Tientsin, 1912

time between the Chinese mutineers and loyal troops under General Chen. The same evening another mutiny, by the Chinese troops in Tientsin, resulted in the destruction of part of the town and continued shooting throughout the night. The European troops spent the night stood at arms.

On 3 March, six companies of Royal Inniskilling Fusiliers were sent to Fengtai to deliver an ultimatum to the rebel Chinese stationed there, demanding they withdraw from the railway station by the following day. Meanwhile, 'E' and half of 'B' Company of the 2nd Batallion, which had been stationed at Fengtai, were sent to Peking to reinforce the Legation Guard.

Second-Lieutenant George Molesworth describes the events of late February and early March in his diary:

Feb 29th … Got to bed about 10.30pm but could not sleep. About 11pm roused up by man of AOC who had been on last train to Peking. Said he had been fired on at Tongchon Junction and forced to retire. Turned out and sent him to get four boxes of ammunition off his truck of stores and bring them in…

March 1st … 12.10am. Shooting began in Fengtai. First a few shots then continuous firing. Pulled on a coat and ran out to the guard room where I found the Colour Sergeant. Ordered the alarm to be sounded. Went back and woke Sale Hill and got dressed quickly. Sent the troops to their alarm posts and served out ammunition … The Chinese fired a field gun behind the station the shell passing high overhead. Ran out to see if I could see the burst but there was none. The parapet was struck by two bullets. At the station the guard had sent up to Wandlow's house to bring him down. He was on a train with all European women and children. They came down but were stopped twice by Chinese troops … About 2.30pm the firing slackened, only desultory firing being kept up all night. The Chinese were evidently looting as we could hear the noise and shouting in the village … Waddy and I went out with a section to reconnoitre. We found the station smashed to bits and the whole village looted. Firing was still going on in the village around. Nothing was touched in the European houses or loco sheds but $7000 had gone from the station…

March 2nd … The Colonel left by the down mail at 5.15, after ordering us to put a 1/2 company permanently on the station. His train was fired on as it left … I was returning with Rigby from his house and coming under the Cannel Bridges saw a big crowd of Chinese troops beating the gunner and his friends. 300 gunners in the Coolie Barracks at once ran for their rifles and opened fire on the crowd … General Chen arrived with

The British post, Fengtai

The British Concession, Tientsin

A scene of rioting, probably Peking

The after effect of rioting, probably Peking

*an escort and while the situation was being explained to him by the officers
in charge of the patrol a few shots were fired at him ... A report then came
in that the gunners were going to fire their field guns at the 'up' mail due
at 6.20pm and having derailed it, would loot it. The Railway telegraph
was smashed, so we wired on the military wire to Langtang to stop the
train...*

March 3rd *... We were ordered to pack up at once and go on to Peking
to reinforce the Guard ... We got to Peking about 9.20pm and met Watts
with an escort and 11 carts. He was fearfully excited about 6 companies
of mutinous troops who were supposed to be sleeping in a train on the
'down' platform. They afterwards turned out to be 50 unarmed looters,
who we saw led away by two armed police. They were afterwards executed
outside the Chien-Mew.*

The Chinese Cavalry, Fengtai, Feb. 1912

The tensions of February and March 1912 eventually subsided, although
mounted infantry patrolled the Chinese areas of Tientsin for several
more days. For the next year and a half the Battalion spent their time
on training exercises and on limited peace-keeping duties before
embarking for India on 20 October 1913 where they were to remain
until the third Afghan War.

Although the time spent in China was short, only two years, and little
active service was seen, the experience was a new one for the Regiment.
This was the only time in its history that it would visit China and its role
was significantly different from what had gone before. Although garrison
duty had been carried out throughout the British Empire, from Gibraltar
to India to Burma, it had always been to provide a British presence in the

area. Here, for the first time it acted as part of an international peace-keeping force in a country not incorporated into the British Empire; it would provide an invaluable experience for duties undertaken during the latter half of the twentieth century.

The Fengtai garrison

Trooping the Colour, Tientsin, 1912

CHAPTER 6

THE GREAT WAR
1914–1918

THE WESTERN FRONT

On 4 August 1914 the Kaiser's German army swept into Belgium in the first thrust of the Schlieffen Plan, aiming to encircle Paris. Consequently a 'state of war' existed between Britain and Germany from midnight and Britain began to mobilise her armed forces, for a war that it was thought would be over by Christmas.

A general map of the Western Front

Within weeks, the two regular Battalions of The Somerset Light Infantry plus the 3rd (Reserve) Battalion and 4th and 5th (Territorial Forces) Battalions, had all been mobilised. In August 1914 the 2nd Battalion was stationed in India, where it would remain for the duration of the war, as one of a nucleus of regular battalions left there in case of any 'troubles'. The 1st Battalion, under Lieutenant Colonel Swayne, was stationed at Colchester as part of the 11th Infantry Brigade of the 4th Division; the 3rd and the depot troops were at Taunton; the 4th (Territorial Force) Battalion was headquartered at Bath and the 5th (Territorial Force) Battalion at Taunton, forming part of the South-Western Infantry Brigade of the Wessex Division. This is not the place to describe every battle and conflict in which the Regiment was involved during the Great War, there being several volumes already which discuss this; instead the major battles which played a key part in the winning of the war and in distinguishing the Regiment will be described.

The men of the 1st Battalion were the first to see active service. Within days of the declaration of war they were mobilised, and within two weeks were in France. They would remain in France and Flanders until the armistice was declared in November 1918. The British Government, thinking that the war would be short-lived, had decided to dispatch only four divisions (1st, 2nd, 3rd and 5th) with the Cavalry Division to form the British Expeditionary Force. The 4th Division, of which the 1st Battalion was part, was ordered to relocate to Harrow to await reservists and further orders. On 21 August the division was ordered to Southampton for embarkation to France to join the British Expeditionary Force. Within a day of its arrival in France the 1st Battalion went into action, stationed astride the Solesmes–Briastre road near Le Cateau ensuring the safe passage of the cavalry. On 26 August the Battalion was involved in the Battle of Le Cateau, hoping to stop the German advance, before becoming embroiled in the retreat from Mons. A day during the retreat from Mons is described by Lance-Corporal Arthur Henry Cook (later RSM, DCM, MM, BEM), a soldier who fought with the 1st Battalion from arrival in France until he received a 'Blighty' wound just days before the armistice:

> **Sun Aug 30:** *Marched about 10 miles … The heat was stifling during the day, however we stuck it mile after mile, God only knows, our throats are parched with heat and dust and every few minutes halt is spent in a sleep of exhaustion. We are too far gone to look or converse with anyone, we are moving as in a dream, every now and then one drops down and another falls out on the side of the road, too exhausted to go another yard, nobody notices him, perhaps he will die of exhaustion, perhaps he will get picked up, more often he is taken prisoner. Our feet are red raw and full of blisters, our limbs are numbed for the want of rest, all life and interest in things seems to have gone, we keep going, how, we do not know … Some of us try to keep in our*

disciplined formation, but it is hopeless, there are no signs of my section of fours, we are getting along in one rabble. Refugees are mixed up with us, old men and women fleeing from the invaders, with their sole belongings in an old pram or trolley, or else on their back. It is a pitiful sight to see them, especially the young mother with the child in her arms and a couple of tots hanging on to her skirts. Sometime a Tommy will help her along, or carry the small child when it is as much as ever he can do to get along himself. Equipment is being thrown away daily by the exhausted soldiers to try and lighten his load … I am keeping my full kit, the overcoat is very useful at night, to cover oneself with … We had a tot of rum and got down to sleep at 11pm, alongside the road. I was dead tired and slept like a top.

The retreat from Mons lasted until 5 September, when the British Expeditionary Force reached its halting place south-east of Paris. The first month of the war was one of exhausted soldiers fleeing from the German cavalry, whilst trying to mount half-hearted counter-attacks to try to buy their comrades some time. The Battle of the Marne in early September halted the retreat and ended the German Army's advance; it was one of the turning points of the war. Although mainly a French affair, the 1st Battalion played a small part in the Battle of the Marne; as part of a large infantry force on the flank of the French 5th and 6th Armies, the 1st Battalion advanced behind the cavalry driving the German Army backwards. On 15 and 16 September the Battalion engaged in the Battle of the Aisne, which was a complete British success and resulted in very few casualties amongst The Somerset Light Infantry.

Soon after the Battle of Aisne the 1st Battalion for the first time entered the trenches which on and off would be their home for the next four years. The early trenches normally consisted of a ditch about 2 feet deep, with little defensive sandbagging or dugouts. For the 1914/15 winter the 1st Battalion was based south of Ypres in Ploegsteert Wood, commonly known as 'Plug Street' by the soldiers. It was a fairly quiet winter with the Battalion taking part in the Battle of Armentières, where they captured the village of Le Gheer from the Germans, and on 19 December, in an attack on the German 'Birdcage'. One of the most notable events of the winter is described by Arthur Cook:

Sun Dec 27: Had to demolish our shelter this morning to allow the R.E.s [Royal Engineers] to build up a breast work. There is no firing to our front. The Germans and our fellows are walking about outside the trenches quite free and easy. A lot of our fellows went out and met Fritz who came half way, a lot of hand shaking took place, followed by exchange of cigarettes for cigars and then paired off and walked up and down No Man's

Land. I went out myself later on and had a chat with several of them, quite a lot of them can speak fair English. I had a cigarette off one of them, they all look well and told us as long as we don't shoot, they won't, so I don't know who will start the ball rolling here again, it is quite amusing to look on the scene and to think that a few hours ago, they were at one another's throats and probably in a few hours time they will be again, they tell us they don't want to shoot. There appear to be plenty of Germans here, by the number knocking about. During this truce here our fellows took advantage of and picked up all our dead which had been lying in No Man's Land since Dec 19, and buried them in the cemetery in Ploegsteert Wood near to Somerset House [Bn. HQ].

The spring of 1915 was, like the winter, fairly quiet for the Battalion, until April when the Germans launched their first gas attack, which led to the second Battle of Ypres. On 22 April the Germans, aiming to mask the movement of troops to the Eastern Front, bombarded the town of Ypres, before releasing chlorine gas over the French front line. At the time of the attack, the Somersets were in billets and it was not until 25 April, after the Battles of Gravenstafel Ridge and Julien, that they were called into action.

A machine gun emplacement in Ploegsteert Wood, winter of 1914

Path making in Ploegsteert Wood, winter 1914

The building of a breastwork, Ploegsteert Wood

Number 1 breastwork, Ploegsteert Wood, winter 1914

Inside Ploegsteert Hall, a dugout in Ploegsteert Wood

Ploegsteert Hall from the outside

The bombardment of the French lines combined with the gas attack had
caused the French forces to flee, leaving a Canadian division to hold the
line. They too were attacked with gas, so that by the time of the arrival
of the 11th Infantry Brigade on 25 April there was a gap in the front line
near to Gravenstafel and Fortuin. It was into this gap that the 11th
Brigade, the 1st Battalion with it, was placed. The Somersets entered
the trenches on the night of the 25th and immediately started to dig in
but due to a lack of entrenching tools, by daybreak the defences were still
shallow and provided protection only if the soldiers lay flat in the mud.
At dawn the Germans spotted the Battalion and immediately their line
was bombarded with artillery shells, which lasted throughout the day. In
addition, the enemy strafed the support trenches with fire ensuring that
no reserves could be sent up. Nothing could be done by the soldiers of
the Battalion except hope for the best and keep their heads down. As
darkness fell, two companies of the Somersets were withdrawn and the
Rifle Brigade reinforced the line; an attack on the two withdrawing
companies was half-hearted and easily repulsed. The day had resulted
in 40 casualties and the rest of the night was spent in building and reinforcing defences. Over the next days the enemy lines were slowly
drawing closer to the British and it was clear that the Somersets would
soon be holding a line clearly exposed and open to enemy fire. On 1

May the French launched an attack to regain the ground they had lost during the initial German attack; if the attack failed the 11th Infantry Brigade was to be withdrawn as the position would become too exposed. The following day the 1st Battalion came under renewed bombardment by enemy fire until late in the afternoon when the Germans unleashed more chlorine gas. It floated directly towards the positions held by 'A' Company, causing 35 casualties. Under the cover of the gas cloud, the enemy advanced to within 200 yards of the British front line. With no substantial advance by the French troops during their attack, the 11th Infantry Brigade was ordered to withdraw on the night of 3 May, but during that day the enemy again advanced and by nightfall was just 70 yards away from where the Somersets lay, making any withdrawal perilous. Luckily, the enemy held their fire and a strong easterly wind helped to protect the brigade's withdrawal.

Over the next month the Battalion again became involved in the second of the Battles of Ypres; first in the Battle of Frezenberg Ridge from 8 to 13 May and then the Battle of Bellewaarde Ridge from 24 to 25 May. Both were typical of many throughout the war, with the Battalion being thrown into the front line to plug a gap whilst being bombarded with artillery and shellfire. The Somersets held their own during these battles but nothing unduly heroic occurred.

On 21 May 1915 the 6th Battalion of the Somerset Light Infantry arrived in France, to be joined two months later by the 7th Battalion. The 6th, having been raised in August 1914, had spent the next nine months training in England as part of the 43rd Infantry Brigade of the 4th (Light) Division. It would remain in France and Flanders for the duration of the war. The Battalion entered the trenches for the first time on 11 June on the Bailleul–Neuve Eglise Road, before moving to Poperinghe at the end of the month. The 7th Battalion, also raised in the summer of 1914, formed part of the 61st Infantry Brigade of the 20th (Light) Division of Kitchener's 2nd Army. Again, until its arrival in France, the Battalion spent its time in training. On 10 September another Somerset Light Infantry Battalion arrived in France, this time the 8th. Formed a year earlier, the Battalion had spent its time training as part of the 63rd Brigade; it would be in France just fourteen days before coming face to face with the German Army.

On 25 September 1915 the Battle of Loos began, which saw considerable participation by the 8th Battalion and subsidiary action by the 6th and 7th Battalions. The main aim of the offensive seems to have been to break the enemy's front and to prevent the re-establishment of his defences; the French had failed in an attack on Vimy Ridge and it was time for an Allied success. During the Battle of Loos the 8th Battalion formed part of the XI corps which was held in reserve and it was only on the second day of the battle that the reserve forces were put into action. The men of the 8th Battalion were deployed along the Hulluch–Lens Road, where they were attacked by the enemy and forced to retire to front-line trenches, which in turn were held until the next day. The day's fighting on 26 September had seen 29 killed, 163 wounded and 91 missing.

Meanwhile, the 7th Battalion carried out fire demonstrations in the front line, aiming to distract enemy attention from the main battle, with the order to go over the top if they looked like running away. The enemy was active throughout the night so the Battalion stayed relatively safely in the trenches, until relieved on the night of 26 September. The 6th Battalion was involved in something more active and costly. The 42nd Brigade, of which the 6th was part, was ordered to capture the Bellewaarde Farm position on 25 September. Two days earlier 'A' Company had moved up to the front line, whilst the other companies were to remain in the Headquarters line. The Somersets held the line all day, whilst other battalions attacked the enemy positions. The next day was spent rebuilding and strengthening the trenches and the 27th remained uneventful, with relief coming the next day. The Battle of Loos was the first encounter with the enemy for these three Somerset battalions and although the experiences were different, they all performed well and helped add to the Regiment's reputation as a fearless fighting force.

The next actions seen by the four battalions of the Somerset Light Infantry in France and Flanders were the Battles of the Somme, between July and November 1916. On 1 July 1916 the great British offensive, known as the first Battle of the Somme, started. At 7.30am 14 British divisions climbed out of their trenches and steadily walked towards the German lines. The attack stretched across an 18-mile front, which wave after wave of British infantry crossed. The object of the Somme offensive was twofold: to relieve German pressure at Verdun, which had been attacked in February, and to assist both the Russians and Italians by tying up German troops on the Western Front. Preparations for the attack were long and arduous; supplies of ammunition, food and water had been stockpiled, transport links were improved, medical stations were constructed and defences were improved. In the week preceding the attack, the German lines were heavily shelled in an attempt to cut their communication lines and destroy their defences. The 1st Battalion was

A map showing the Battles of the Somme, 1916

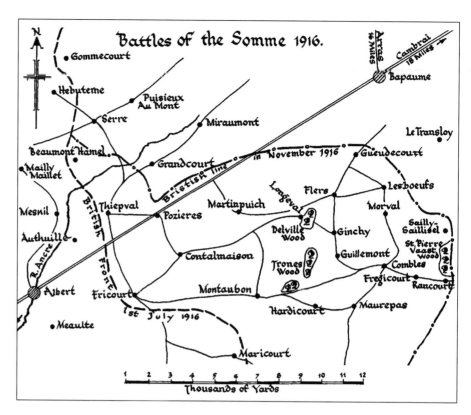

involved in the opening scenes of the battle which would last five months. It was deployed at Mailly Maillet, and it was from here it made its attack on 1 July. Arthur Cook details this day in his memoirs:

It is a lovely morning and the birds are singing ... The bombardment is now terrific the German lines are one cloud of smoke, that it seems to be impossible for anyone to live in such a hell, it's a wonderful sight. We were able to stand on the parapet to get a better view, there is not a sign of life in front and no response from the German Artillery, we have that to come I expect. The men are in excellent spirits and eager to make a move, after being so long in the trenches. At 7.20am a huge mine was exploded under the Hawthorn Redoubt just to our right front, it made our trenches rock. Punctually at 7.30am the attack was launched, the R.B.s [Rifle Brigade] led the 11th Bde attack. Troops could be seen advancing in perfect skirmishing order, as far as the eye could see left and right. What a sight it was to watch, everything going smoothly with no resistance, the first line had nearly reached the German front line, when all at once machine guns opened up with terrific murderous fire. Our men were timed to advance 10 minutes after the R.B.s, but so eager were they to get on, that they left soon after the R.B.s, and consequently were caught in the open by these guns. A and B Coys were the leading Coys followed by C and D in close support. M.G. [machine gun] fire was directed on us from both flanks, men are falling fast just like skittles, my platoon officer, 2Lt [Second Lieutenant] Tilley has fallen, also platoon Sergeant, this leaves me now in charge ...

this within 5 minutes of our advance ... I led the platoon into the German first line, and after a breather went into the German second line, here I lost control owing to the men rushing from one shell hole to another in their advance. The ground is littered with our dead ... The clearing parties are not doing their work properly in clearing the trenches of all Germans, as here and there parties of Jerrys are popping up and throwing grenades at us from all angles ... it is impossible to get any further, it is said some reached their objectives and are now cut off from us ... Col Hopkins of the Seaforths is doing excellent work here, he is walking around giving encouragement to all, he saved a dangerous situation when someone gave the order to retire, there was an immediate panic and some 4 or 5 hundred retired, it was a very difficult job to stop the whole lot retiring and it was only by a bugler of the Seaforths sounding the 'charge' that saved the situation ... I have never seen so many dead in such a small area before, in places where enfalade [enfilade] fire caught them they are 3 and 4 deep on top of each other, the shell holes are full of wounded and no hopes of getting them back ... The Germans were now trying to force us out of their trenches, we got together what was left of us now and by collecting bombs from the dead and what Jerry left behind we managed to hold on for another 2 or 3 hours, then the supply of bombs gave out and no more could be got, the Germans then gradually drove us back inch by inch through their superior supply of bombs, again someone gave the order to retire and again men started to retire, we stopped this as every man was wanted in the trench, We are a very small number here now and men are being killed and wounded in all directions, it is difficult to walk in the trench without walking on the dead ... I have a terrible thirst caused by the fumes from the shells, the wounded are also crying out for water, but none is available ... the sight is terrible, nothing but dead and wounded all around you ... Our troops are gradually retiring leaving a very small garrison to hold the trench ... now we have to retire to the German front line and try and hold that with the rifle and machine gun, but it is bombs we want, as Jerry is bound to advance up the communication trenches ... This is getting pretty hot here now but our orders are to hang on to what we have until midnight, when we are being relieved, but we seem to be about the only British troops around here, my party numbered 9 men. I think I can hold these people as long as the bombs last, but when they are gone, I don't know what we shall do ... The enemy artillery has now started and are dropping shells thick and fast all around us ... We held on until relieved about 11pm, an officer then said we may go back, we didn't need telling again, we had had our belly full ... As soon as we started to go back Jerry dropped a barrage in No Man's Land ... The night got blacker and blacker after each blinding flash ... I jumped from shell hole to shell hole, fell head-long over dead bodies and barb wire, my clothes was being torn to ribbons, I thought I should never

An anti-aircraft machine gun

A French gun destroyed by shellfire, c.1914

reach our trenches and when I did I fell in sprawling not being able to see them in the dark. The next thing I saw was a form standing over me with a bayonet pointing in a threatening manner at me, I began to wonder if I had got into Jerry's trench, I should not have been surprised if I had, but it was OK, it was a British sentry, he thought it was a German came tumbling in, as he had received orders there were no British troops in front, I had a very narrow escape there from being shot by our own men.

A 17-feet deep shell hole, near La Brique

The first days of the Somme, also known as the Battle of Albert, lasted from 1 to 14 July. On the first day 26 officers and 478 men of the 1st Battalion were dead, missing or wounded for no immediate gain.

Among the dead was Brigadier General Prowse of the 11th Infantry Brigade and formerly of the 1st Battalion.

The 8th Battalion also took part in the Battle of Albert; as the action began the Battalion entered the trenches east of Becourt Village and at zero hour on 1 July they crept over the top and across No Man's Land. The advance was met with heavy machine-gun fire and casualties were heavy, especially amongst the officers. Undeterred, the Battalion reached its objective and began to infiltrate the German front lines and communication trenches, where they remained for the night of 1 July. A counter-attack was expected but none materialised. On 3 July the Battalion again advanced and held these new positions until relieved the next day. The Battle of Albert had caused the death of ten officers and 425 other ranks were killed, wounded or missing.

Aerial view of the German front lines at Beaumont Hamel

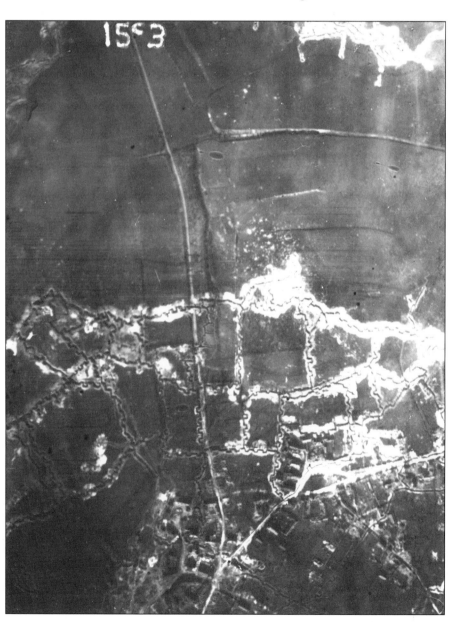

The two remaining battalions were also soon to become embroiled in the Battles of the Somme. On 12 August the 6th Battalion found itself fighting for Delville Wood, an area which changed hands many times during the summer of 1916 and which changed from a beauty spot to a hideous place to fight, with bushes and tree stumps providing innumerable places for the enemy to hide. Upon entering the trenches the enemy's position was unknown and the nerves of the battalion were stretched to breaking point. On 16 August it was engaged in fighting along the north-east side of Delville Wood, a battle that was easily won. The 7th Batallion became involved in early September, with the Battle of Guillemont. The enemy's position around the village of Guillemont was strong, riddled with deep and well-built defences. On three previous occasions, British forces had attacked the village, but because of problems defending their flanks, the position had had to be given up; the 7th was to help in the fourth attempt. The attack began on 3 September with orders to capture Guillemont, clear it of German troops and secure the main road. The 7th performed well; its objective was achieved and the line of the main road held until the Battalion was relieved.

The next of the Battles of the Somme was the Battle of Flers-Courcelette, which saw the first use of tanks in active combat. The 7th Battalion was ordered into action on 16 September, with the objective of capturing and holding the German front lines. The attack was carried out superbly, a front of 150 yards was taken and fifty prisoners captured, with the loss of 172 men of the Battalion. The 6th also joined the fight that day, with the order to attack the German trenches in front of the village of Gueudecourt, the final objective. Unfortunately, a lack of reconnaissance meant the wrong trenches were occupied and thus the objectives of the battle were not achieved. The Battalion's losses on this day were terrible; every officer became a casualty, and of the other ranks, 41 were killed and 203 wounded.

October 1916 saw the Battle of Le Transloy Ridges, which marked the end of involvement in the first Battle of the Somme by the 1st and 7th Battalions. The ridges were part of a series that lay along the Somme and which provided the British with considerable strategic advantage, affording control of the high ground. Of the two Battalions, the 7th was the first to become involved; the aim of the 61st Brigade (of which the 7th was part) was to push out patrols and secure a good jumping off point from which to attack the German trenches. This would mean that the 7th would have to cross No Man's Land and dig in immediately in front of the enemy's trenches. Despite this, the operation was entirely successful, with few casualties. Six days later the men were again ordered to push forward to construct a reserve line in support of an attack. Their task was then to mount a follow-on attack should the leading battalions be successful. The attack was successful and the Battalion carried out its orders to the letter, with few casualties. It was not until the last day of the battle that the 1st Battalion became involved. It was to attack in co-operation with the French, who were targeting the village of Sailly-Saillisel. Heavy rain dogged its efforts, making the ground slippery and hard-going, and trench-foot was rife, but the Somersets held their ground and over the next few days enemy gun emplacements and ground were captured.

The final clash of the Battles of the Somme involving The Somerset Light Infantry was the Battle of the Ancre from 13 to 18 November. This battle saw the 8th Battalion holding trenches west of Beaucourt and establishing strong points to help an attack on the German line. The attack failed and the Battalion had to withdraw. Between June and November 1916 the British Army lost 415,000 officers and men during the Battle of the Somme. In total the Royal Artillery had fired seven million rounds on the Somme between July and September: an astonishing total which helped to contribute to the wishes of a quick strike by the enemy at the beginning of 1917.

The winter was spent by all four Battalions in tours of duty in and out of the trenches, until the spring offensive of 1917 began. That year marked a fresh initiative by the Allied leaders who wanted to put the losses of the Somme behind them. The Germans also wanted to strike quickly and try to bring about a victory. Thus the year saw all the Battalions of the Somerset Light Infantry heavily involved in France. In March 1917 the German Army had withdrawn to the Hindenburg Line, also known as the Siegfried Position: it was a defensive line which lay 25 miles behind the existing German lines on the Somme and was heavily reinforced by concrete and miles of barbed wire. In addition the land in front of the Hindenburg Line was cleared of features such as wells, roads and railways, in order to stop the quick establishment of the Allied front lines. The Hindenburg Line provided a shorter German front, which would save the hard-pressed German Army's 13 divisions, and it was hoped that the increased defences would help prevent battle losses on a par with those of the Somme.

The Battle of Arras, like the Somme, contained many smaller conflicts, the first of which was the first Battle of the Scarpe from 9 to 14 April. This was an attempt by the British to divert German attention away from the Aisne in order to relieve pressure on the French. The plan involved slightly fewer men than deployed for the Somme and the attack was over a smaller area; the results, however, speak for themselves. The German second line was captured with ease and with the loss of 32,000 casualties, compared with 57,470 on the first day of the Somme. Arras represents an interesting first for The Somerset Light Infantry, with all four Battalions (the 1st, 6th, 7th and 8th) involved, although the 7th only took part in the flanking operations.

In the opening stages of the battle, the 6th Battalion, as part of the 14th Division, was in the front line, with the 8th and 1st in reserve, ready to leap-frog the lead battalions after the initial attacks. At 5.30am on 9 April 1917 the attack was launched, under a heavy barrage of artillery fire and within forty minutes of the opening attack the German front lines were captured. The 6th on its advance met little opposition at first, with two platoons capturing a machine gun and 30 German prisoners. It then consolidated its position and waited for the battalions on its flanks to catch up. The next attack was met by heavy machine-gun fire, which led to heavy casualties amongst the leading company. By night-fall the 6th was ordered to consolidate its positions. Meanwhile, the men of the 8th had been waiting out the day of the initial attack until sunset. They were then ordered to advance to Orange Hill, a crest lying 500 yards from the German trench system, and to consolidate their positions. The 1st Battalion's objective was the German third trench system, which ran from the river Scarpe through Le Point du Jour, and then to pass through the captured trenches and attack Vimy Ridge, where the fourth line of German trenches lay. Its objectives were seized and many Germans, shocked by the heavy artillery, surrendered. On the first day of the battle all three Battalions of The Somerset Light Infantry were involved, achieved their objectives and consolidated their positions. The next few days for the 6th and 8th were just as successful as they kept up their attacks, and by the 13 April both Battalions were back in billets. For the 1st Battalion its involvement was to last a little longer. On 11 April it launched an attack on the German lines. It was met by heavy machine-gun and rifle fire and little ground was gained. The weary soldiers were finally relieved on 14 April after suffering days of shellfire and constant attacks.

The second Battle of the Scarpe followed closely on the heels of the first. The French launched their attack on the Aisne and the weather began to improve, allowing the next step in the Arras offensive to be taken. On the morning of 23 April, the Allies attacked along a 9-mile front. The 8th Battalion, as part of the 37th Division, was given the objective of

A group of German prisoners, taken 9 July 1915

capturing the Roeux–Gavrelle Road. It was swept with heavy machine-gun fire and suffered heavy casualties, but managed to hold the position until it was relieved during the night. Just four days later the 8th Battalion was again called into action, this time taking part in the Battle of Arleux, the sole purpose being to help the French. The line of the British attack was 8 miles, with additional activity at each end to give the impression of a much larger attack. Once again, the objective was a road, the Plouvain–Gavrelle Road, and with the attack timed at 3am the night was so dark that confusion reigned; the Somersets swung to the left and their objective was only partly attacked, although successfully. However, mopping-up parties became isolated and it was some time before the Battalion was fully relieved.

The 1st and 6th Battalions became embroiled again in May, with the launch of the third Battle of the Scarpe. This was one of the closing confrontations of the Battle of Arras. The aim of the attack was to distract German attention and tie up reserves from an attack launched by the French on the Chemin des Dames. The 1st Battalion aimed to capture the village of Roeux, whilst the 6th remained in divisional reserve throughout the battle. The 1st's attack was launched at 3.15am on 3 May and was immediately stalled by heavy enemy fire from Roeux Woods, which an artillery barrage had failed to dislodge. The Somersets managed to fight through the wood and reached the western outskirts of the village, but were unable to consolidate their position as they were too few in number and enemy fire was too heavy. The attack failed and the soldiers withdrew to the British trenches, with a loss of three officers and 132 other ranks, killed, wounded or missing.

July and August 1917 saw a return to Ypres for the third battle, with the 7th and 8th taking part in the battles of Pilkem and Langemarck. The hope was that this would bring about the decisive victory that the Battles of Arras and Aisne had failed to achieve. The main offensive began on 31 July and it was on this day that the 8th Battalion joined the fight, in the Battle of Pilkem. The aim of the 37th Division was to help extend the line of attack in order to spread enemy counter-fire, and at the same time to create the impression that a serious attack was planned for the Warneton-Zandvoorde Line near Hollebeke. The 8th Battalion formed part of the second phase of the attack, which was heavily contested and was initially successful but with many casualties. On 16 August, the 7th took part in the Battle of Langemarck. The conditions were terrible. Four days of steady rain had turned the ground into a treacherous mud bath making operations virtually impossible. The Battalion was placed in the front wave and, as with the 8th's attack during the Battle of Pilkem, the attack was a success, but again casualties were high.

Whilst the 7th and 8th were involved in these battles, the 1st Battalion spent the summer in and out of the line recovering from the losses sustained during the Battle for Roeux. In October it took part in the Battle of Broodseinde and then in the Battle of Poelcapelle. The former lasted for only one day, 4 October, and involved both the 1st and 8th. At 6am the attack began and was met by ineffective enemy machine-gun fire. The first German trench was occupied with little resistance; the second objective, a road heavily fortified by machine guns, was less easily captured. The third objective, Ferdan House, was heavily defended, but ultimately captured with 30 prisoners. The Battle of Poelcapelle followed five days later on 9 October. For the days between the two battles it had rained steadily, so the ground was in a terrible state but nevertheless the attack was launched at 5.20am, without postponement. The 1st Battalion remained in Divisional Reserve ready to be called forward as reinforcements, but was not needed. Poelcapelle marked the end of the involvement of the Somerset Light Infantry in the third Battle of Ypres. They did not become involved in either of the battles of Passchendaele but remained behind the lines providing a support network of working parties.

With the end of the third Battle of Ypres the Allies started to look for a new area of attack, and the town of Cambrai in Picardy was chosen. It was to be a unique battle as it was the first in which the Allies used tanks in large numbers, and to a positive effect. At the time, it was important for the Allies to keep up the attacking initiative. Russia and the Eastern Front had collapsed and German forces were flooding toward the Western Front. America had not yet mobilised its forces and the French forces were suffering severe problems with morale, and heavy losses. The constant attacks in Flanders had meant a weakening of German defences in other parts of the line, making Cambrai an ideal place for a surprise skirmish. Thus the great tank battle that formed the first stages of the Battle of Cambrai began on 20 November. In the battle plan, the tanks were intended to smash through the enemy defences, clearing a path for the infantry to follow. The line of attack stretched along a 6-mile front, lined with six divisions of Allied forces and 420 tanks. The 20th Division (containing the 7th Battalion) was on the right of the line between Villers Plouich and La Vacquerie. The Battalion's objective was to capture of the village of La Vacquerie, a key position protecting the right flank of the attacking forces. The 7th

Battalion were allotted nine tanks, three for each attacking company, and had 1200 yards to cross before reaching the German lines. The first stages of the attack went well and within an hour, the village was reported cleared of enemy troops, with very few casualties. At 2.30pm the Battalion was ordered to advance again, but by now it had begun to rain and the passage was a sea of mud littered with broken tanks and guns, necessitating a long detour on higher ground before finally reaching the objective. On 21 November it was once more ordered to advance, across a footbridge over the canal. This was achieved and its objectives were again met, with few casualties. In the initial attack on Cambrai the 7th Battalion had performed splendidly, with all objectives secured and minimal casualties. However, on 30 November the Germans launched a counter-attack.

A tank cemetery near Ypres, Belgium, 1920

The Cloth Hall, Ypres, Belgium, showing shell damage, 1920

The 7th Battalion was in the front-line trenches when the Germans greeted dawn with a heavy barrage followed by a line of attacking infantry. The 7th defended well and cut a path through the attacking Germans with machine-gun and Lewis gun fire, but ammunition began to run short and the battalion on the right of the Somersets had fled, leaving the path clear for the enemy. Orders for a withdrawal were given and each time a stand was made the enemy overran it. By the end of the day the 7th Battalion had been all but wiped out; only two officers and about 60 other ranks remained, with losses of 12 officers and 332 other ranks. It was a terrible blow for both the Battalion and the Regiment that a battle which had started so well should end so badly, with so many deaths.

What was to be the last year of the war, 1918, dawned. It was a year featuring a strong offensive by both sides, which would lead ultimately to the collapse of the German war machine. In March the German Army launched its spring offensive, aiming to defeat or be defeated, before their resources ran out. This offensive saw all four Battalions again involved in fighting before being augmented by the 11th and 12th Battalions in May and the 2/4th Battalion in June. With the launch of the German offensive in the Somme in March, the 6th and 7th Battalions were immediately called into action. On 21 March in the Battle of St Quentin, the lines held by the 6th Battalion were swept first by mustard gas and then by heavy shelling, which cut all communications leaving the front-line troops isolated. The German infantry swept across No Man's Land and reached the British front lines without warning. The 6th Battalion suffered badly in the attack, and only four men out of 560 made it back to Brigade headquarters. The 7th Battalion fared little better, when in a German attack on 23 March it suffered heavy losses and a day later at the Somme Crossing was forced to retire in the face of heavy enemy action. Between 23 and 25 March the 61st Brigade, of which the 7th Battalion was part, suffered such heavy losses that, on the 25th, it was reorganised into a composite battalion of four companies. The total strength of this unit was nine officers and 440 other ranks, barely the size of a normal battalion.

On 5 April the Germans launched a heavy attack on the whole front, north of the Somme from Bernancourt to Bucquoy, but gained little ground thanks to the defensive actions of the 37th Division and the 8th Battalion. The German offensive coincided with a planned attack by the Allied forces, which aimed to straighten out and strengthen their line. The Allied attack, involving the 8th Battalion was fairly successful, but it was forced to withdraw because of a loss of communication. A counter-attack by the enemy was beaten off, apart from a small sector where the enemy surrounded the troops there, capturing 20 Somerset men whose rifles were clogged with mud. A total of 161 men were killed, wounded or missing at the end of the day.

The war clouds also began to gather in the north. On 7 April the Germans let loose a heavy bombardment of artillery over the Allied lines between Lens and Armentières; two days later the bombardment started again and was followed by a wave of attacking German soldiers. The attack infiltrated the lines of the Portuguese, just west of Aubers. Wave after wave of fresh German soldiers poured over No Man's Land to be met by worn-out and depleted numbers of Allied troops. To stem the German advance to the north, reserve divisions were brought up from the south, amongst them the 4th Division, which included the 1st Battalion. On 12 April the 1st entered the trenches north-east of Lillers. It was here that it became involved in the Battle of Hazebrouck.

The objective was the village of Riez du Vinage and the establishment of a line from the village southwards to join with the canal. In order to carry out the attack they had to first cross the canal, which meant a risky daylight assembly at the bridges. The attack was launched at 6.30pm and was met by vigorous enemy fire, but nonetheless the companies swept towards the village and by 7.15pm it had been secured. The next evening it was ordered to help to capture the Riez-le Cornet Malo road, which again was achieved. The two days' action had seen the recapture of 21 Allied guns and the taking of 135 German prisoners.

The German offensive ground to a halt. In late spring and early summer, the Allied armies started their offensive which would lead to the ending of the war. The counter-offensive began south of the Aisne, its success leading to plans being formed for the Allied advantage to be pushed along the northern part of the Western Front. However, none of the Somerset Light Infantry Battalions in France, now increased to seven with the addition of the 2/4th, 11th and 12th, were to take part in this great push to victory and it was not until 21 August that the 8th Battalion became involved in the second Battles of the Somme.

At 4.55am the 1918 Battle of Albert began. The 8th Battalion, as part of the 63rd Brigade was to attack on the left to capture and consolidate the high ground and to shatter the enemy resistance. The 8th's objectives were achieved quickly and easily, with few casualties; 60 prisoners and six machine guns were captured. This position was consolidated and held, then the Battalion moved forward securing the village of Bihucourt. On 26 August it took the quarry north of Bihucourt, before being relieved at the end of the day.

Meanwhile, the 1st Battalion had been following the German withdrawal in the Lys Valley. On 26 August the Battle of the Scarpe began. The 1st was not involved in the opening stages of the attack but moved into the front lines south of Boiry Notre Dame on 28 August to carry on the advance. The following day the attack was a success and the enemy was driven back. On 30 August it was detailed to attack the town of Eterpigny, which was captured with neither effort nor difficulty. In the next push, the Battle of Drocourt-Quéant line of 2–3 September, the objectives were again easily achieved and the enemy capitulated with little resistance. The final two confrontations for the 1st Battalion, the Battle of the Selle, 17–25 October and the Battle of Valenciennes, 1–2 November, were neither historic nor momentous battles; on both occasions the enemy gave little resistance and their objectives were secured. After the Battle of Valenciennes, the 4th Division, including the 1st, was withdrawn from active service.

Meanwhile, the other battalions had been fighting their way to an Allied victory. In August, the 8th and 12th became involved in the second Battle of Bapaume at the end of August and the 12th fought in the Battle of Epéhy on 18 September, both low-key affairs. Between 8 and 9 October the 8th was involved in fighting during the Second Battle of Cambrai. Luckily it did not suffer the losses experienced a year earlier by the 7th. Here the Battalion displayed great perseverance and courage fighting successfully in open country, a form of fighting previously little used during the war. From this point on, the remaining Battalions of The Somerset Light Infantry in France were involved in the pursuit of the enemy; the 8th taking part in the Battle of the Sambre of 4 November, the last battle of the Great War, which forced the Germans to sue for peace.

What has been described here is a series of battles and lesser actions often in appalling conditions with horrific casualties. However, battalions did not spend all their time in the trenches. There were periods out of the line spent in billets, on training and acting as working parties. The soldiers and especially officers were granted periods of leave, both in France and at home, and there was time for recreational activities such as hunting and battalion games. Arthur Cook describes an occasion where the men were given relief from a constant source of irritation – lice:

> ***January 1915:*** *This was a very quiet month and not much to write about … it was a period of mud and water trenches in 'Plug Street' Wood, alternating with brief spells at Nieppe and handing in our accumulation of lice over to the officials in the brewery where we had our periodical bath in the beer vats. It is rather interesting the procedure we had there, the Coy [Company] would march there and undress in one very large room with the exception of our vest and shirt, our serge was rolled up in a bundle and pushed into a great fumigator, everything had to be taken out of the pockets, especially leather as that would come out all shrivelled up and snap like a carrot. We used to then line up with our boots in our hands and wait till a vat was clear and in the period of waiting we used to be killing the lice of the man in front of you. As soon as a vat was ready off would go a dozen of us, though the door, out on to the canal path in full view of everyone for about 20 yards into the vats and there we would carefully put our boots where we could keep an eye on them, as good boots were in the habit of disappearing, and take off our shirt and vest and into the vat, just think of a dozen soldiers splashing about in a beer vat and there was plenty of room, some men were scratched all over where the lice had irritated them, but no one took any notice we were at war and at the time in a lovely hot bath, as soon as our time was up we were ordered out by the froggies, where we got towel, shirt and vest waiting for us and as soon as we were dried and got our shirts on, we jumped into our boots and ran along the canal into the first room, where pants were issued and we got our serge out of the 'oven' all steaming and hot and creased lovely all over (I don't think). We used to look a sight, but we were happy, we left fresher and there was prospects of a night's sleep without any scratching.*

THE MIDDLE EAST

The Western Front was not the only arena of war in which The Somerset Light Infantry fought. Whilst the 1st, 6th, 7th and 8th Battalions were fighting through the mud and throwing themselves against the German defences, and the 2nd Battalion marched from garrison to garrison in India, the 1/5th, 1/4th, 2/4th, and 12th (formerly West Somerset Yeomanry) were engaged in a totally different form of battle in the Middle East. Although the Great War had started as a European war, fought on European soil, the ripples of conflict began to spread. With the consolidation of the alliance between Japan and Britain, attacks were made against German ports in China, whilst South African forces invaded German territories in Africa. The Middle East also soon developed as a theatre of war that was to see the use of 1,200,000 British and Colonial troops; with the sheltering of two German destroyers in Constantinople in August 1914 the Germanic influence soon began to spread through previously neutral Turkey. British and Colonial troops poured into Egypt in order to protect the strategically important Suez Canal and the routes to India from the Turks in Palestine. They were also sent to Basra to protect the Persian oil fields in Mesopotamia.

During 1914 the 1/4th, 2/4th and 1/5th Battalions, which had been raised by splitting the pre-war 4th and 5th Battalions into two battalions each, sailed for India, where they trained and prepared themselves for war. It was these Battalions which would fight for The Somerset Light Infantry in the Middle East. Towards the end of February 1916 the 1/4th Battalion landed at Basra. Before its arrival General Townshend's forces had failed to take Baghdad and had retired to Kut-al-Amarah where they were under siege. The first attempt to relieve the town, in January, had caused a Turkish retreat, but the town still remained besieged. The 1/4th, as part of the 37th (Indian) Infantry Brigade, was sent to Basra as part of a relief force to rescue Townshend's troops and to ensure protection for the much-needed oil of the region. On the night of 24 February, the Battalion began its journey upriver towards Kut-al-Amarah, and on 7 March was involved in the capture of the Dujailah Redoubt. This was its first action. It performed well, but the British forces were forced to withdraw. For the next month the Battalion was involved in further attempts to relieve the besieged town, but rain made the fighting conditions difficult. In April the besieged forces inside Kut-al-Amarah surrendered having run out of food supplies. On 2 May the 37th Brigade was relieved and returned to Basra. Ill-health forced the Battalion to take no part in the return to Kut-al-Amarah or in the advance to Baghdad at the beginning of 1917. Instead it spent the rest of the war in localised actions in and around Basra.

A view of Amarah, Mesopotamia

The year 1917 saw an increase in activities in the Middle East. Things were not going well in France and Flanders and the British War Office felt a victory in other theatres would provide a huge propaganda and morale boost. An offensive was launched in the Balkans, attacks on Baghdad increased and the British offensive to capture Jerusalem began. The first Battle of Gaza, of March 1917, saw a bold frontal attack on the Turkish garrisons in Gaza. This failed thanks to a lack of organisation. The second Battle of Gaza began just three weeks later and saw the involvement of the 12th Battalion. Formed from the 1/1st West Somerset Yeomanry which had fought at Gallipoli, the 12th had come into being in January 1917. The Battalion had moved to Ismailia in December 1916, and in January it moved to El Ferdan on the Suez Canal, then in March towards El Arish where the British forces were concentrating. After the failure of the first Battle of Gaza, all reserve forces in the area were called forward to help defend the front. The second battle was set for 17 April, but the 12th remained in reserve throughout and the attack, a full-frontal attack, again failed.

The summer heat meant a break in operations in Palestine, but with the coming of autumn, the third Battle of Gaza began, this time involving the 1/5th, 2/4th and 12th Battalions. The attack this time, struck at the

A view of Basrah city, Iraq

coastal areas around Gaza, but at Beersheba, which lay at the Eastern end of the Turkish line, allowing the British cavalry to attack the rear of the Turkish forces. The 12th formed part of the 74th Division, whose aim was to attack the defences north of Beersheba if needed. The 1/5th and 2/4th battalions, part of the 75th Division, were engaged in holding the line in front of Gaza in order to protect the main attack on Beersheba and draw enemy fire. The attack was timed for 8.30am on 31 October. The first objectives were soon captured by the attacking divisions and by 12.15pm the British forces were targeting Beersheba, a complete surprise to the Turks who expected the traditional attack on Gaza. The action was so successful that no call was made on the reserve forces of the 74th Division. From 1 November the British forces began to assemble for the attack on Jerusalem. On 6 November they targeted the Turkish Kauwukah trenches, with the southern portion being allotted to the 74th Division, who started the operation. The 12th Battalion launched the assault at 5am and was met by heavy machine-gun fire. The Turkish trenches were deep and well prepared, and the British had to advance over 4000 yards of open ground with no cover. The operation was well-executed and by 7.15am the Battalion had gained its first

Right and below: *Turkish mines and guns captured at Shaiba, Mesopotamia*

objective, capturing 63 prisoners and 14 guns; the second objective was gained by 7pm. These successes were paid for heavily by the Somersets, who having started with 700 men, saw 42 killed and 197 wounded.

Elsewhere, the other Battalions were attacking Gaza. The date and time of the assault had been left open depending upon the progress of the main attack on Beersheba. The success of this led to the date for Gaza being set for 2 November at 3am. The 75th Division, including the two Battalions of the Somersets, were on the right. The attack was almost an immediate success, with almost all objectives reached. Neither the 1/5th nor the 2/4th were actively involved in the fighting, either being in

reserve or holding other sectors. In the following week, the 1/5th Battalion helped to push forward and ensure the collapse of Gaza and the acquisition of abandoned Turkish supplies, whilst the 2/4th remained stationed behind the lines.

It was now a classic pursuit, with the Turks retreating and the British chasing after them, pushing their advantage. A few skirmishes occurred on the way in which the 1/5th was involved. In just fifteen days the British forces had marched 60 miles and had divided the Turkish Seventh and Eighth Armies. The next objective was Jerusalem. The Turkish Seventh Army had retreated to the city and it was placed upon the Somerset men of the 75th Division to try to remove it. In the first attack, the battle of Nebi Samwil, the plan was for the 75th Division to be in the centre of the assault and to seize the Bab el Wad defile. The operation was begun on 17 November 1917 by the Cavalry Divisions and two days later, the infantry started its advance. Enemy action was easily opposed, but the terrain made the going slow. In an assault on the village of El Jib north of Jerusalem, on 22 November, the Division met stiff resistance causing heavy losses and making it necessary to withdraw. The attack began again the next day, but once more losses were high, with the 1/5th suffering 221 casualties, and orders for another withdrawal were issued.

It was then the turn of the 12th Battalion to take part in the attempt to capture Jerusalem. Between 27 and 30 November the Turks had

Turkish prisoners captured at Shaiba, Mesopotamia

A bivouac in front of Gaza

A caravan about to set off to fetch the daily supply of water

A canteen and dugout at the apex of the British lines in Gaza

'D' company of the 1/5th Battalion bivouacked on the way to Gaza

Turkish shells bursting on the 1/5th Battalion, Gaza

Turkish guns captured by the 21st Corps during the final attack on Palestine

launched a series of counter-attacks and so plans for the final capture of the city were hastily prepared; roads and tracks were improved, supplies and ammunition were stockpiled and the water supply was ensured. The date of the attack was set for 8 December, and with the 74th Division attacking from the west (with the 12th Battalion in reserve), the plan was to surround the city. Turkish resistance to the initial assault by the 74th Division was fierce and the Division advanced only 4000 yards. On the 9th the reserve battalions were moved closer to the front in expectation of fierce fighting, but the Turks surprised the British by surrendering the Holy City, depriving the 12th of the honour of helping seize the city. With the capture of Jerusalem, the British no longer needed many troops in the area. By the end of April 1918 the 12th had received orders to prepare for service in France.

Throughout the first half of 1918, the 1/5th and 2/4th Battalions were involved in local operations in Palestine. However, Turkey was by no means out of the war and Palestine was still partly occupied by the enemy. In September and October the final offensive for the capture of Palestine took place. The 2/4th, like the 12th had been sent to France, arriving in June 1918, so the only Somerset Battalion left in the Middle East was the 1/5th. On 19 September the Battle of Sharon began, with the Battalion moving in to the front line on the night of the 17th to hold positions along the Hadrah Road. Immediately, patrols were sent into No Man's Land to cover preparations for the attack. Two companies from the 1/5th (Nos 2 and 3), attached to the 234th Brigade, were tasked to capture the most advanced Turkish positions; the other companies of the Battalion to hold the front line until the arrival of the main body of troops. Nos 2 and 3 companies advanced at 4.30am, and within fifteen minutes had secured their objectives with no casualties. The day resulted in the overwhelming of the Turkish Eighth Army, with the Seventh Army in full retreat although already surrounded. An armistice was signed with Turkey on 31 October 1918, making the attack on 19 September the last active operation by the 1/5th in the Great War.

At the eleventh hour of the eleventh day of the eleventh month of 1918, the war was over. The Somerset Light Infantry had fought hard throughout the four years in France, Flanders and the Middle East and had gained 72 battle honours in some of the most horrific but also most famous battles of the war. Throughout the conflict, one Victoria Cross was awarded, to Private Sage, and over 600 other bravery awards were received. Some 4756 Somerset Light Infantrymen are listed in the

Golden Book of Remembrance in Wells Cathedral. It was a tremendous sacrifice, not only by the men of The Somerset Light Infantry, but by the men of the British Empire, and one which would be repeated only twenty-seven years later.

Private T.H. Sage, awarded the Victoria Cross for most conspicuous bravery during an attack by the 8th Battalion on an enemy strong point on 4 October 1917, at Tower Hamlets Spur, east of Ypres. Sage was in a shell hole with eight other men, one of whom was shot whilst throwing a bomb. The live bomb fell into the shell hole, and Private Sage with great courage and presence of mind, immediately threw himself into it, thereby saving the lives of those around him whilst causing himself extensive injuries

CHAPTER 7

THE INTER-WAR WORLD

THE THIRD AFGHAN WAR

The third Afghan War came hot on the heels of the Great War. It was only a small border tussle, but it saw the Somersets again visiting the country where they had gained their most famous battle honour. The reasons for this conflict had echoes of the 1842 war. Since the second Afghan War of 1878–79 there had been an uneasy peace between Britain and Afghanistan. Russian influence in the country had eased for a while but was renewed in 1900, and an agreement made in 1907 reinforced Russia's acceptance of British interests in Afghanistan. During The First

An unidentified Afghan fort

World War Afghanistan remained neutral mainly thanks to heavy British subsidies, and despite interference by Germany and Turkey. However, with the end of the war, once again came Russian interest. In 1917 Tsarist Russia had been overthrown in the October Revolution, to be replaced by a Communist government headed by Lenin who had pledged to further the cause of International Communism. At first the USSR was concerned with internal affairs and reorganising the country along Communist lines, but behind this lay the wish to gain security against any further European conflicts and so began a system of peaceful penetration into weaker states.

The spark for the third Afghan War was the assassination of Amir Habibullah Khan, the country's leader, on 19 February 1919. With the support of the Afghan army and the Young Afghan Party, his third son Amanullah was installed as Amir of Afghanistan. Amanullah was suspected of killing his father, so to divert attention from himself he declared a jihad against Britain on 3 May 1919, hoping to exploit the growing anti-British feelings in India. In March rioting had broken out throughout the Punjab and on 13 April 1919 a group of Ghurkha troops had been ordered to fire on an unarmed crowd in Amritsar. Hoping to fully exploit the outcry over this incident and the scarcity of British troops in the North-West Frontier area of India, Amanullah intended to retake the North-West Frontier Province, which had been lost to Sikh expansionism during the 1820s.

The Amir's camp, Bali, Rawal Pindi, c.1900

Throughout the Great War the 2nd Battalion had been stationed in India and had thus missed the conflict, but now it was in a prime position to participate. Operations ranged along much of the border between India and Afghanistan, with fighting in Chitral, the Khyber Pass, the Kurram Valley, the Tochi Valley, in Waziristan and in Baluchistan. The 2nd Battalion was in action at the Khyber Pass and around Bagh and Dakar; on both these occasions the Somersets were victorious and the Afghan army was driven back. When the British advanced into Afghanistan the Battalion was ordered to march to its old battleground of Jellalabad, but a lack of transport led to a change of plan and the advance was called off. An extract from the war diary of the 2nd Battalion explains the action around Loe Dakka:

This gun was taken by no. 2 platoon, 'A' Company, 2nd Battalion from the 'regular' Afghan army at the action fought at Loe Dakka on 17–18 May 1919.

The enemy throughout 17–18 May had held the ridge, Sikh Hill-Stonehenge Hill (changed after the action to Somerset Hill) in great strength, and earlier attempts to dislodge them had resulted in considerable casualties to Indian army units and had been unsuccessful.

This gun, the only one on the ridge, which was otherwise held by a cloud of riflemen, had been a considerable nuisance the whole time, although a high percentage of its shells had bounced rather than burst!

On the evening of 17th May, the 2nd Bn which had been in reserve and was the last card in the Commander's hand, leaving 'B' Company to hold the ford over the Kabul River, was ordered to capture the ridge.

The three companies attacked on a two platoon front with 'A' Company leading, No. 2 Platoon being the right platoon. It was extremely hot and the climb exhaustingly steep.

About twenty yards from the summit we paused for a moment to get our wind, and then went over in a solid rush.

No. 2 Platoon rushed over and round the gun, the Afghans did not wait and were about a hundred yards down the rear slope, running for all they were worth and were severely mauled by the rifle fire of the Bn. as they streamed away.

The Battalion consolidated their position on the hill and held it all night suffering tremendously from thirst, but they had hit the Afghans so hard that, otherwise they were undisturbed.

The war lasted only three months, with the Treaty of Rawalpindi, signed on 8 August 1919, marking the end. This treaty recognised Afghan independence, with Britain guaranteeing that its Indian empire would not extend past the Khyber Pass; British subsidies to Afghanistan also

Left: *A view from India looking through the Khyber Pass to Afghanistan, c.1915*

Below: *The 2nd Battalion marching through the Khyber Pass at the end of the war*

ceased. It was a small conflict, but nevertheless resulted in another battle honour for the 2nd Battalion, with 'Afghanistan 1919' being added to its Colours. After the fight for Dakka, the hill formerly known as Stonehenge Hill was renamed Somerset Hill, a permanent reminder of the Regiment's actions in Afghanistan. It was on this hill that the Battalion's buglers spurred on their comrades to action, probably for the last time during active service.

The Headquarters dugout during the fight at Dakka, 17 May 1919

The interior of Green Hill piquet, the outer line of defences, Dakka camp, May 1919

Shells exploding during the conflict

The Afghan peace delegates

Regimental crests cut into the rock at Cherat near Peshawar, 1904

An advertising poster for the Regiment, c.1925

Regimental sports, Lahore, 1913

The result of a partridge hunt, Delhi, c.1920

CHAPTER 8

THE SECOND WORLD WAR
1939–1945

The year 1914 had seen the eruption of the largest and most horri-fying war ever; just twenty-five years later, another exploded which was to surpass the first in terms of involvement and overall deaths. The causes of the Second World War are common knowledge and need no discussion here, but the ripples sent out by the conflict were to reverberate throughout the rest of the twentieth century and would help to dictate the role that The Somerset Light Infantry would play henceforth.

On 3 September 1939, following the invasion of Poland, the British declared war on Germany. At this time the 1st Battalion was stationed at Poona in India, and the 2nd Battalion at Gibraltar. As in the Great War the Regiment increased dramatically in size from two battalions to ten, six of which saw service overseas. The first six months of the war, known as the Phoney War, saw little action by the British Army; instead resources were put towards defence and in readying and enlarging her small peacetime contingent. But the defeats soon started. At the end of May 1940 the British began their withdrawals from Dunkirk and Norway, and by 25 June France had fallen and Italy had entered the war; defences in Britain were stepped up to guard against an expected invasion. In August the conflict spread to Africa and the threat to British interests there and especially the Suez Canal increased.

During the first months of the Second World War, the 1st Battalion at Poona, under the command of Lieutenant Colonel A.F. Harding (later Field Marshall the Rt. Hon. the Lord Harding of Petherton, GCB, CBE, DSO, MC, undoubtedly the Regiment's most distinguised officer), acted as Frontier Defence Reserve. In the spring of 1940 it was involved in operations in the Ahmedzai Salient on the North-West Frontier. In Gibraltar the 2nd Battalion, which was under the command of Lieutenant Colonel O.G.B. Philby, found conditions in the early stages of the war much akin to peacetime, and its war diaries were not begun until

A 2nd Battalion Guard of Honour at Government House, Gibraltar, 28 July 1941

The officers of the 1st Battalion, Waziristan, India, 1942

early in 1941. At first, the Battalion was employed in strengthening the defences and providing guards for shipping. Throughout 1939 and early 1940, the 4th and 5th (Territorial) Battalions were mobilised, the 6th, 7th, 8th (Home Defence) and 11th (Holding) Battalions were raised and a Somerset Light Infantry Brigade (135th Infantry Brigade of the 43rd [Wessex] Division) was formed. Circumstances drew these newly formed Battalions towards southern England, where they were engaged in home defence and preparations for an expected German attack.

The 4th Battalion motor transport lines, Exmouth

THE WAR IN BURMA

The first sustained active service by The Somerset Light Infantry came in 1943 with actions by an understrength 1st Battalion in the Arakan, a western coastal province of Burma, 60% of its experienced personnel having been drafted to other theatres of war. With the Japanese attack on Pearl Harbour in December 1941, the conflict had spread to another theatre of war. The attack on the American Pacific Navy had coincided with similar raids on British-held positions in the Far East including Hong Kong and Singapore. Japanese forces swept through Asia and by March 1942 British forces were evacuating Burma. To the British it seemed that the next step for the Japanese would be India.

A Bren gun in action during a 4th Battalion exercise on Exmoor

The 7th Battalion transport section, September 1941

At this time the 1st Battalion was part of the 114th Indian Infantry Brigade of the 7th Indian Division. The British plan of operations for the winter of 1943/44 was to secure the frontiers of Bengal and Assam, to occupy North Burma, opening a land route to China and to advance into the Arakan. The 7th Indian Division entered the Arakan in the autumn of 1943 towards the end of the monsoon season. On 25 September the 114th Brigade began to move into the Kalapanzin Valley to close in on the Japanese. Throughout October, the Division continued 'closing in' on the enemy, improving communications and stockpiling stores. In early October intelligence indications were received that the Japanese forces were thinning out, and it was decided to drive home the advantage and try to isolate Japanese forces as they withdrew. The plan of attack was to push southwards forcing the enemy to retire, and only attacking, when necessary, those positions still held by the enemy. On 1 December Operation Cotton was launched; this aimed to cut off the westerly of three fingers of a hill feature behind Awlanbyin, which was strongly held by the enemy. The attack met little opposition and by late afternoon, the feature was cleared. The 1st Battalion was involved in checking and clearing a feature called 'the bone'. This was achieved easily, but an encounter with the enemy the next day forced the attacking companies to withdraw. Towards the end of December, it was noticed that the Japanese were no longer using the main road in the Arakan as a supply route, nor were they making any attempt to stop British patrols in the area; a general advance was thus ordered.

The 1st Battalion took part in Operation Hook, the objective of which was to cut off and destroy enemy garrisons between the Kalapanzin and the Arakan Yomas foothills. It was an ambitious action, with five separate phases; in addition, Japanese positions had complete observation of the whole area. On 15 January the 1st Battalion was moved to the northern end of the Pyinshe Ridges and enemy attacks on patrols began immediately. Progress by the 114th Brigade was in the face of heavy opposition, the Japanese being determined to stop the advance at all costs. They were spread out widely through thick and difficult country, the front about 5 miles long, interspersed with defensive bunkers. On 23 January the 1st Battalion was ordered to take a strong point on the southern end of Pyinshe Kala Ridge. Reconnaissance that night was poor because of thick mist and the operation was postponed for twenty-four hours. It was a difficult position to attack; a switch-back track had been cut along the top of the ridge to help patrols, ending in an almost perpendicular drop of 80 feet, followed by a similar rise to the enemy position. On the east the ridge fell cliff-like to a stream and was impossible to climb without ropes, while the southern end of the ridge around the enemy position was thick with jungle. The only path of attack was on the south-west side, a steep convex slope, also covered with jungle. The attack began at 0600 hours on 26 January. Just 30 yards short of their objective the leading platoon came under heavy automatic and grenade fire at close range; the fallen men made it even more difficult for the other platoons to advance. Orders were given to dig in, but the following platoons had bunched up and confusion reigned. Attempts to send up supplies of ammunition and at the same time to work in from other angles along the ridge were thwarted by enemy fire. On the evening of the 26th all the men were dug in and reporting that if ammunition was sent up they could hold the position for another twenty-four hours. Several attempts were made to get the ammunition through but they either became bogged down in paddy fields or the mules in the mule train bolted. Throughout the night of 26/27 January the enemy harassed the 1st Battalion's position; the next day another offensive was planned but Japanese fire and a frontal attack forced the Battalion to withdraw. Deaths and casualties for this operation totalled 70 men.

Towards the end of January the Japanese launched a counter-offensive to drive the British back up the Arakan. It seems that they intended to try to cut off the 7th Indian Division and then destroy it. Under the cover of darkness and mist, the Japanese slipped 800 troops into the area and on 4 February launched a surprise attack on the 1st Battalion's position. With the coming of dawn the situation was utterly confused; an artillery battery firing on the Japanese forced British platoons to withdraw in order to avoid casualties, and all communication lines were cut. The British forces became split up into a series of isolated 'boxes' and found themselves continually harassed by Japanese attacks. Rations were low and casualties high; the wounded could not be evacuated. Despite this, the British held their ground, and by the end of February the Japanese began to give ground, and the Allies were again able to push their front line forward. Throughout March the 1st Battalion was involved in skirmishes and attacks on the Japanese before, on Jellalabad Day, being sent back to India for reorganisation and a rest. It was not to return, but for the rest of the war remained in India on garrison duty. The actions in Burma had been very different from the Burmese wars its predecessors had fought. There had been no easy victory.

THE WAR IN THE MEDITERRANEAN

In the European theatre of war little had been happening for the Battalions of the Somerset Light Infantry, but, with American entry into the conflict, plans for the invasion of Europe began in earnest.

Russia and America favoured a full attack on France, as it would provide the quickest route to Germany and thus the quickest end to the war. Churchill, fearful of defeat and ever a Colonial, favoured an attack on the 'soft underbelly of Europe', through Italy and the Mediterranean. Two battalions were involved in the Italian Campaign, the 2nd and the 30th.

The 30th Battalion had started life as the 8th (Home Defence) Battalion. After spending the first years of the war in various defence duties in Somerset, in December 1941 the battalion was redesignated as the 30th. Intensive training and home defence were now undertaken, until orders for service overseas were received on 6 August 1943. On 23 September the Battalion reached Algiers and on 29 October, as part of the 43rd Infantry Brigade, moved to Sicily. On 14 March 1944 orders were received to prepare for a move to Italy. Arriving there on 12 April, the Battalion was engaged in train and railway protection for the 8th Army. It was eventually disbanded two years later.

By early 1943 the 2nd Battalion was still on defence duty in Gibraltar and the men were beginning to feel like their predecessors in the First World War, that they would miss out on real action. However, in April and July the Battalion was sent in two batches for intensive training at

A group of warrant officers and sergeants from the 30th Battalion, Rome, 1945

Les Andalouses in North Africa. In early December 1943 orders came for the Gibraltar Brigade, of which the 2nd Battalion was part, to move to Egypt. Once there the Brigade was renamed the 28th Infantry Brigade and became part of the 4th Infantry Division. The first months of 1944 saw the 28th Brigade carrying out intensive training, to catch up on the five years' battle training missed whilst in Gibraltar. Great secrecy surrounded the Brigade; mail was still to be addressed to Gibraltar and for security reasons the 4th Division was known as the 34th Division. It was believed that it was to be part of a secret landing somewhere in the Mediterranean. This proved not to be the case, and in February orders were received for the Division to move to Italy. Upon arriving there the Battalion was first stationed in the village of Le Vogie, near Naples, where the bombing of Cassino was clearly audible. In just days it would be much closer to the fight.

The situation in Italy at the time saw two attacking Allied fronts; the US 5th Army, which included British formations, was moving northwards along the west coast towards Rome, and the British 8th Army was stretched across the Appennine Mountains to the Adriatic coast, occupied in clearing up Southern Italy. The 4th Division became part of the American 5th Army and took part in operations in the Garigliano Valley. The 2nd Battalion's first experience of active fighting was patrols on 21 March 1944, in which the enemy was engaged. At the end of March the 4th Division transferred to the British 8th Army in the south.

At the end of March 1944 the 2nd Battalion was ordered to join a detachment consisting of the 56 Recce Regiment of the 13 Corps; this detachment was responsible for holding a long section of the front, known as the Valvori sector. On 29 March the Battalion billeted in the village of Pietra Vairano, which lay 10 miles south of the front. Both the village and the road leading to the front were under heavy shellfire, and the route was passable only at night. On the night of 2 April advance parties of the Battalion began to move forward to occupy positions on the summit of a high ridge which fell steeply to the river Rapido at the rear and into a valley at the front. The enemy positions, mainly Austrian, lay just 1000 yards beyond the valley. Whilst in the front line the Battalion experienced several skirmishes with enemy patrols, resulting in several deaths. On 15 April it moved to the Belvedere Sector, holding a position with clear views of Monastery Hill at Cassino. Preparations then began for the spring offensive, which aimed to link up the 5th and 8th Armies near the Anzio beachhead, before launching a large-scale attack on Rome.

The overall operation, which would lead to the advance on Rome, was known as Operation Honker, although each division involved in the attack used different names for its part in the action. The 4th Division was to cross the Garigliano River, to establish a beachhead and then, in conjunction with the 5th Army, advance on Rome. The attack by the 4th Division was key to the whole operation as the sector included Highway 6, the main route to Rome. On the night of 10 May the Battalion moved into its positions, ready for the attack; zero hour was fixed for 23.45 hours on 11 May. At 2300 hours the artillery barrage opened, covering the valley in a thick smoke. The river crossing by the lead battalions, the 2nd King's Regiment, had not gone well; the current was stronger than anticipated and mortar fire had knocked out many of the boats, while paths through a minefield had become congested by Engineers' vehicles. Two hours late, at 0400 hours, the Battalion completed the river crossing, but on reaching the road immediately came under heavy fire. Things were going equally badly for the other party of the Battalion crossing the river, as it had sustained many casualties from enemy fire and many of its wireless sets had been knocked out. Disorientated by the darkness and smoke, platoons were losing touch with each other. A mistaken order led 'B' Company to withdraw from the river to the boat assembly point. The Commanding Officer, Lieutenant Colnel Platt, was wounded and isolated for thirty hours. On 12 May no movement was possible under the intense mortar and sniper fire. No further troops made it across during the night and it seemed that the enemy was closing in on the small bridgehead. Events turned when on the morning of 13 May the Engineers managed to construct a bridge able to carry tanks across the river and thus relaunch the attack. By 1400 hours, the enemy had begun to surrender and the Battalion pushed forward. The 4th Division was then pulled out to rest. In total, 12 other ranks were killed, and 141 men were missing or wounded. The town of Cassino was taken by British troops on 18 May and the monastery was stormed; that same day Highway 6 was cut. Five days later the attack from the Anzio beachhead was launched. On 4 June American troops entered Rome.

However, Italy had not yet fallen. The mountain range down the middle of the country made communications between the coasts difficult; the terrain was more suited to the defender than the attacker. A shortage of equipment and men made landings behind enemy lines difficult and the enemy had ensured that all bridges over the many rivers had been demolished, causing delays in crossing them. With forces called away to help in other theatres of war, it was a delicate situation. In early June the 4th Division, as part of the 8th Army, was fighting on the flank of the 5th Army heading northwards. On 23 June the 2nd Battalion took part in an assault on the town of Vaiano. The advance was strongly opposed; attacking at

1000 hours the first push by the Battalion was received by heavy enemy fire and the companies soon began to lose communication with each other. Heavy firing and mortar shelling continued until 1900 hours when the enemy began to retire. The next day the attack continued and on 24 June, the town was taken. During the early weeks of July, the Battalion fought in further skirmishes in the area, which were generally successful.

On 20 July the Battalion took part in the advance on Florence. At first, there was little opposition, but on 25 July the enemy's defences began to stiffen and the going became tough. However on 4 August the southern outskirts of the city were entered and the enemy started a full retreat. The fall of the city was a serious blow to the Germans but they were able to fall back to a prepared line, the Gothic Line, which stretched along the Appennine Mountains in the west, to carry on their defence. After the fall of Florence, the 4th Division moved south near to Foligno, then on to the Adriatic sector. The Battalion then took part in the advance to the Ausa River on 14 September and the Marecchia River on 21 September. October saw the crossing of the river Savio, then the Ronco River in November, and on the 22nd an attempt was made on the Cosina River. The 2nd Battalion had to secure a bridgehead before swinging north, aiming for Faenza. After a successful initial crossing came a counter-attack, but it was held off and a slow advance was achieved. This was to be the last action seen by the Battalion in Italy. Greece had meanwhile reached boiling point and the 4th Division was transferred there, the 2nd Battalion embarking on 26 November.

From 1940 Germany had started to send troops into Greece, despite a neutral Turkey blocking her path to the east. By having bases in Greece, Germany would be able to attack shipping in the Mediterranean and strike at bases in Palestine and Egypt. In 1939 Britain had given guarantees of support to Greece and was thus honour-bound to uphold them. When pressures from other quarters forced the German army to begin a withdrawal in September 1944, landings of British forces followed. But the new Greek government outlawed the Communist guerrilla groups who had been fighting the Germans, and rioting broke out, which would lead to civil war. It was into this volatile situation that the 2nd Batallion landed. Their first action was protecting traffic on the Piraeus–Athens road in December 1944. In January they moved on to clear Athens of guerrilla forces. Both actions were achieved, with few casualties, and by 8 January fighting in Athens had ceased. The Battalion remained in Greece until early 1947 on peace-keeping duties and assisting the Greek forces to counter Communist insurgents; it was then transferred to Austria.

Above and below: *The 2nd Battalion in Kavala, Greece*

THE WAR IN NORTHERN EUROPE

The main theatre of war for the European campaign was France and the D-Day landings, and The Somerset Light Infantry played its part in this key fight. Three Battalions of The Somerset Light Infantry fought during the Allied offensive in France and Germany, the 4th, 7th and 10th Battalions. The 4th, a territorial battalion, received orders to embody on 25 August 1939 and spent the next four years in home defence and training. The 7th Battalion was formed from the 5th (Territorial) Battalion in August 1939, and it too spent the next four years in home defence and training. The 10th Battalion was raised in 1940 and like the others also spent the early years in home defence and training. On 2 November 1942 a letter was received by the War Office offering conversion to a parachute battalion or disbandment. 450 men of the old battalion volunteered to join the parachute battalion and by 8 November, the 10th had become the 7th Battalion (Light Infantry) the Parachute Regiment.

Between 28 and 31 May 1944 the three Battalions received orders for their part in the coming battle for Normandy and the years of training were about to be put into practice. Operation Overlord, the code name for the attack on the Normandy beaches, had two phases: to assault and break up the Atlantic Wall and then to link up the beachheads and build up the forces for a break-out. D-Day was set for 6 June 1944. On the night of 5/6 June airborne landings were carried out by the 82nd and 101st US Airborne Divisions in the Cotentin Peninsula, in the west, and by the 6th British Airborne Division, in the east. The 7th Battalion (L.I.) Parachute Regiment, part of the British 6th Airborne Division, took off from Fairfield airfield in Kent at 2320 hours on 5 June, and at 0050 hours on 6 June they began to drop near Ranville in France. Many loads were dropped in the wrong place and one was not dropped at all, meaning that the Battalion went into action at less than one-third strength and without wireless sets, machine guns or mortars. By 0325 hours it had reached its objective of Le Port and Benouville, but was heavily counter-attacked. At 0015 hours on 7 June the 7th was relieved and moved to brigade reserve; odd parties who had got lost in the landing joined through the day. In this first action 19 men were killed, 42 were wounded and 170 other ranks were missing.

At 1330 hours on 7 June the Battalion occupied a defensive position near the hamlet of Le Hom. The seaborne section provided reinforcement the following day whilst the rest of the Battalion was under heavy attack near Le Hom. It spent 9 June holding these positions and the next day attacked woods close to Le Mesnil. On the 13th the Battalion took up positions at Herouvillette. Here it was heavily attacked, with several casualties. On 17 June it carried out a successful raid on a farm, which led to the capture of six German prisoners. The Battalion subsequently remained in the line until early September, advancing as far east as Pont Andemer on the River Isle. On 3 September it embarked in the SS *Empire Jardin* at Arrorranites, and docked at Southampton on 5 September.

The 4th and 7th Battalions, as part of the 43rd Wessex Division, did not take part in the D-Day landings but were sent to France once the beachheads were secured. Rifle companies sailed from Newhaven and the vehicle parties from London docks. The 4th Battalion landed at Arromanches and the 7th at Courseulles. Both then marched to concentration areas, the 4th at Ryes and the 7th at Rucqueville. The battle for Normandy had now reached its third phase and the 2nd British Army now had to form a bridgehead over the Odon River. Codenamed Operation Epsom the action took place on 25 June and used the 43rd Wessex Division to force a crossing over the river and gain control of the high ground north-east of Bretteville-sur-Laize, overlooking the roads leaving Caen. The 4th was given a counter-attack role, with the 7th as relief for the attacking battalions. Both spent late June and early July in patrols and small-scale operations.

In early July Operation Jupiter was planned; this was a series of thrusts by the British 2nd Army with the aim of moving southwards along as broad a front as possible. The role of the 43rd Division was to secure the high ground between the river Odon and the river Orne. On 10 July 129th Brigade of the 43rd Division, which included the 4th Battalion, was ordered to attack Hill 112, a rise on the top of a 10-acre plateau, the sides of which sloped gently. The majority of the area was covered with standing corn, and the plateau could be observed from three sides, while the approaches had little cover. For the attack the Battalion was supported by a squadron of Churchill tanks from the 7th Royal Tank Regiment. A and D companies led and C and D companies were in support.

At 0500 hours on 10 July the attack began; although still dark, burning carriers and tanks lit up the scene and the Germans fired on the advancing troops with mortars and artillery. Casualties were extremely heavy and the summit of Hill 112 was not reached. The attack on the hill was the hardest fought and the most bloody of the whole war for the 4th Battalion; the unit which had sailed from England was virtually destroyed. A monument to the 43rd Wessex

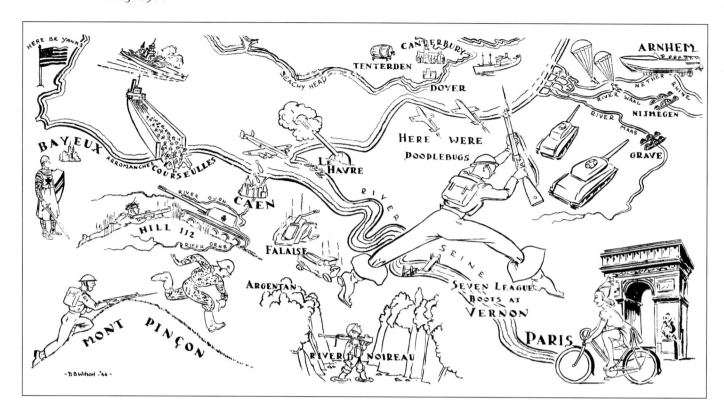

The 43rd Wessex Division's progress across Europe. The image is taken from a Christmas card of December 1944

Division now stands on Hill 112. Sergeant R.H.W. Brew describes the attack on the Hill in his memoirs:

We left our positions and moved cautiously to the bottom of a rise, just over the river Odon, it was a cornfield really, that rose gently into the darkness. It was marked on the map as hill 112, little did we know that it was to become famous, and that it would be awarded to the Regiment as a battle honour.

The big push inland had begun, and it was not a bit like we had thought. The noise was terrific, tanks firing, guns firing, snipers firing, Moaning Minnies coming over, I realised then that I am not a brave man, just very scared. Our mates were going down like nine pins, and all you could do was stick their rifle in the ground, with their tin hat on top to mark their position, so that the medics could find them in the long corn …

… We had nearly made it to the top, when we were ordered to dig in, and Mucky and me did just that, mighty quick or die. The shells continued to rain down, and how we survived I'll never know, for after that battle we had a 192 killed, wounded or missing. It was a terrible price to pay, so many of my mates just gone, we all felt numb but in time we got used to it, there was no reason why it was one bloke and not another, when it was time to go, well, so be it.

Four days in all we were on Hill 112, with no hot food or drink, as the runners couldn't get up to us because of the snipers in the corn. Sergeant Jack Whitting took over the platoon when a shell landed near Sergeant

Bickham's trench, the blast snapped his rifle but left him unharmed, but he was taken back with shock and we never saw him again. We came down from that hill as battle hardened troops, it was something they could never have put us through at battle school.

The 4th Battalion's casualties in the 10 days leading up to and during the battle for Hill 112 were 525 out of 830 all ranks.

The remainder of July saw the two Battalions participating in attacks to break out of the Normandy bridgehead and to push the German front lines backwards. On 30 July the 4th Battalion attacked the village of Briquessard and the next day the 7th Battalion attacked Les Haies. By August, the British Army had regrouped and was ready to attack south-wards into the Caumont area. On 1 August the 43rd Division was directed to take and secure Mont Pincon, attacking at 0200 hours on 3 August. The 7th Battalion remained in reserve on the day of the attack and the 4th Battalion was joined by a tank squadron to attack the hill. The 4th moved up on 5 August but its progress was halted by a blown bridge which took nine hours to repair. At 1230 hours on 6 August the 4th was ordered to attack; the day was extremely hot and resistance was high. The leading platoon of 'A' Company was almost wiped out by auto-matic fire and 'B' Company also sustained heavy casualties. At 2330 hours, a few Churchill tanks of the 13/18 Hussars reached the summit of the hill and another tank was moved into position to fire on to the hill-side. This proved to be the turning point of the battle. The 4th advanced under heavy fire and by darkness 'C' and 'D' companies had reached the summit. On 7 August the 7th Battalion relieved the 4th and consolidated the position.

On 25 August Operation Neptune was launched, to secure a bridgehead over the River Seine. The 4th Battalion was to cross at Vernon and the 7th was in reserve. At 1917 hours the Battalion crossed the river in storm boats and Dukws (amphibious vehicles). At first opposition was light but the first attempt to land was made on an island separated from the far bank by 60 yards of deep, muddy water. It was almost dawn by the time the two attacking companies had landed. The 4th was then ordered to occupy the village of Bois Jerome St Ouen. As it reached it, it was heavily attacked and forced to withdraw, but after confused fight-ing the Germans withdrew shortly after it became dark.

Next came Operation Market Garden. The obstacle to the British 2nd Army was a series of rivers and canals at Arnhem, Nijmegen, Grave and Eindhoven. The main feature of the plan was to drop a 'carpet' of airborne troops on the road Eindhoven–Uden–Grave-Nijmegen–Arnhem, and thus form a bridgehead at Arnhem. The 43rd Division, now part of 30 Corps, was to advance from the river Meuse-Escaut Canal bridgehead, and if the bridges were found to be destroyed the 43rd was to undertake bridging operations. On 17 September 1944 the airborne troops began to drop onto their objectives; at 1425 hours 30 Corps began its advance on Eindhoven, soon breaking enemy resistance. Heavy fighting continued to slow the Allied advance throughout 18 and 19 September and plans were made for 30 Corps to push on with all speed to Arnhem the next day. During this time the 43rd Division was advancing along 'Club' Route threatened by German forces on either side. The Germans succeeded in cutting the Route on four occassions, on 19, 20, 22 and 24 September, on the latter occassion for forty-eight hours. At 2330 hours on the 21 September orders were received from 30 Corps to capture the Arnhem road bridge intact and to make contact as soon as possible with the 1st Airborne Division in the area of Oosterbeek ferry.

At 0700 hours on 23 September the 214th Brigade, including the 7th Battalion, began to attack to clear the main road to Arnhem. They met strong resistance at Oosterhout and from the outset casualties began to mount. A change of plan ensured that the objectives were reached by 1800 hours. The next morning the advance was continued with little opposition and 1830 hours the 7th was dug in on its objectives. Over the next two days they helped capture and hold Elst, a critical point on the Arnhem Road. On the 26 September 129 Brigade, which included the 4th Battalion, relieved the 7th and for ten days the 4th, often under very heavy shelling, drove off German counter attacks. Meanwhile the 7th Battalion was involved in the operation to withdraw the 1st Airborne Division. On 27 September it was ordered to move forward and drive the Germans back over the Nedn Rijn downstream from the Arnhem Bridge. It reached its objective that evening and the next day carried out mopping up operations, taking 145 prisioners of war.

By the end of the Arnhem battle Field Marshal Montgomery's plan was to cross the Rhine and strike at the Ruhr, but because of long lines of communications and supplies, this could not be done until the port of Antwerp had been captured. In addition, the enemy was still holding out near Venlo in country ideal for defence, while the land between the Rhine and the Maas also had to be cleared. Montgomery thus decided to attack in a south-easterly direction from Nijmegen, using 30 Corps. The Germans, however, had recovered from the attack on Arnhem more quickly than expected and were regrouping into a strong force on the Scheldt estuary. It was thus decided to call off the attack. It fell to 30

Corps to defend the flank between the Waal and Maas rivers east of Nijmegen, whilst planning the resumption of the offensive on this front.

In November came Operation Clipper, to clear the west bank of the Maas and to take ground up to the Roer River. The 43rd Division had to attack on the right towards Geilenkirchen. The 7th Battalion, as part of the 214th Brigade, was to break through north of Geilenkirchen and cut the road leaving the town. The attack began on 18 November and by 1430 hours the 7th's objectives were captured. The continuation of the attack on 19 November was postponed owing to a heavy counter-attack to the south; this was held and the clearing of the area continued. On 21 November the DCLI with D company of the 7th Battalion The Somerset Light Infantry captured Hoven but was forced to withdraw the next day under a heavy counter-attack.

By the end of November the Allies had taken Antwerp and supply problems had eased. In December the Allied forces began to regroup for the attack on the Rhineland. For the assault on the Reichwald, 30 Corps was to concentrate on the Nijmegen bridgehead, with a view to driving towards Krefeld. Although timed to start on 12 January 1945, the attack was postponed because of enemy action in the Ardennes in December. By the end of that month, the enemy's counter-stroke had been beaten off and all that remained was to clear up the pockets of Germans left by the counter-stroke before the attack on the Rhineland could begin.

Now 30 Corps was moved northwards towards the Nijmegen bridgehead to join the 1st Canadian Army to clear the Germans from west of the Rhine; the area was the flood plain of three rivers, with wooded country between them. They were to attack the Siegfried Line near Kranenberg and open the road to the higher ground near Cleve, allowing the 43rd Division to pass through the Materborn area, swing round the Reichwald Forest and capture Goch. Operation Veritable, as this attack was called, began on 7 February 1945, although the infantry advance did not begin until the next day and it was not until 9 February that the 43rd Division saw any action. The 129th Brigade had made a breakthrough on the 8th, and now the 43rd moved forward to exploit it. On 10 February 129 Brigade advanced on Cleve believing the town to have been evacuated. The 4th Battalion The Wiltshire Regiment ran into a road block and was fired on, losing several carriers. Once the obstruction was cleared the 4th Battalion The Somerset Light Infantry passed through and by 0700 hours, riding on tanks, had reached the centre of town. A German counter-attack on the town led to confused fighting and the Battalion became split into many small parties fighting

The buglers of the 7th Battalion on parade in Uelzen, Germany

The 7th Battalion parade in Uelzen, Germany

from street to street. Later that day the 214th Brigade moved forward and relieved pressure on the 129th Brigade. On 12 February the 129th Brigade's advance continued, led by the 4th Battalion, with the objective of the village of Bedburg, and by 1700 hours the area had been secured. This had been a 'real' Light Infantry advance to contact.

By 13 February the Reichwald Forest had been secured and it was time for the second phase of the Battle of the Rhineland. On 14 February the 129th Brigade advanced towards Goch but was met by heavy artillery fire. The next day saw a pause in the offensive, with heavy enemy action and bad weather to contend with. On the 16th the 4th was temporarily attached to the 214th Brigade for a further advance, west of the Cleve-Goch Road, with the objective being the high ground on the southern edge of the Reichwald Forest. The attack, by both the 4th and 7th Battalions, began at 1300 hours and by 1720 the latter had reached its objectives. The next day the attack continued with the 4th Battalion moving to the rear of the 7th which was still engaging the enemy. The offensive continued for the next three days, by the end of which Goch was firmly in Allied hands. The first day of March saw the launching of Operation Blockbuster, which captured the Cathedral town of Xanten, with the 7th seeing a significant part of the action. By the 12th the area had been consolidated, although under considerable enemy fire.

By March 1945 Allied forces had reached the Rhine, but it was a considerable obstacle. On the 7th the 1st US Army found a bridge still standing at Remagen and managed to establish a bridgehead on the eastern bank of the river. The next stage in the Allied attack on central Germany was Operation Plunder, which would aim to cross the Rhine, north of the Ruhr on a two-army front, using the British 2nd Army and the 9th US Army. A significant bridgehead would then be formed to allow the build-up of forces for a break-out. The date fixed for the launch of the operation was 24 March. The 43rd Division was in reserve whilst the 51st Division helped to launch the attack across the river. The 6th Airborne Division, including the 7th (Light Infantry) Parachute Battalion, was to drop on the opposite side of the river and disrupt enemy defences north of Wesel. It was dropped over the area at 1018 hours on 24 March and by 1200 hours, all positions were gained. At 0930 hours, the next day contact was made with the Commando Brigades who had led the attack over the Rhine. On 26 March the Rhine was crossed by both the 4th and 7th Battalions, with the latter successfully engaging the enemy. On 27 and 28 March the 43rd Division successfully enlarged the bridgehead, taking several prisoners.

The next step was the break-out from the bridgehead; 30 Corps' task in this was known as Operation Forrard On, set for 30 March. At 1000 hours, the attack was launched, with the 4th Battalion leading. There was slight opposition at Sinderen from a German company supported by a Mk IV self-propelled gun but by 1830 hours Sinderen had been taken and the advance continued. By 0600 hours, the next day the town of Varsseveld was in Allied hands and with little opposition, by 1 April the Brigade was attacking Lochem. The next objective was Bremen. For the first two weeks of April the 43rd Division sped across Germany even though resistance was often stiff. On 24 April 'B' Company of the 7th Battalion opened the road to Bremen and the next day the attack from the south on the city began. On 26 April orders were received to clear Bremen, and the 4th Battalion was held in reserve for this action, but was called forward to take part in the difficult street fighting. During the day Major V.W. Beckhurst of the 4th received the surrender of Major-General Siebel, the 2nd-in-Command of the Bremen defences. By 29 April the city lay firmly in Allied hands.

On 25 April American and Russian forces met at Torgau on the river Elbe; 1 May saw the unconditional surrender of German forces in Italy. The previous day, 30 April, Hitler had committed suicide, and the Second World War in Europe was drawing to a close. The last action by the three Battalions in Germany took place on 1 May. The 43rd Division were ordered to clear the north bank of the river Wumme in the Quelkhorn-Tarmstadt area, with the 7th Battalion in the advance and the 4th in reserve. Little opposition was met. The 7th moved to Bukhusen and the next day occupied Kletzin and Moidentin near the Baltic coast. On 2 May came the unconditional surrender of Berlin to the 1st White Russian Army and by 4 May all enemy forces in Holland, North West Germany and Denmark had surrendered unconditionally. At 0800 hours on 5 May the 'ceasefire' was ordered.

The war was over. Although it had been a slow start for the Regiment, not seeing action until 1943, its battalions had fought in three major theatres of war and proved themselves time and again. In doing so they had fought in different terrains, from jungles under monsoon rains to European forests thick with mud and covered in snow. Lieutenant G.A. Cairns received the Victoria Cross and Private J.H. Silk and Captain Latutin the George Cross all posthumously; 133 other honours and bravery awards were received and 176 Mentions in Despatches. In total 65 officers and 883 other ranks had died during the conflict, as always, a heavy price to pay for victory.

Lieutenant George Albert Cairns was awarded a posthumous Victoria Cross whilst attached to the South Staffordshire Regiment. On 12 March 1944 the South Staffordshire Regiment and the 3/6 Gurkha Rifles established a road and rail block across the Japanese lines of communication at Henu Block. The Japanese counter-attacked the position and the South Staffordshire Regiment were ordered to attack a hilltop that formed the basis of the Japanese attack. During this attack, Lieutenant Cairns was attacked by a Japanese officer who hacked off Cairns's left arm with his sword. Cairns killed this officer, picked up his sword and continued to lead his men in the attack. Lieutenant Cairns later died from his wounds. Cairns had joined the Somerset Light Infantry in 1941 and was attached to the South Staffordshire regiment whilst in India

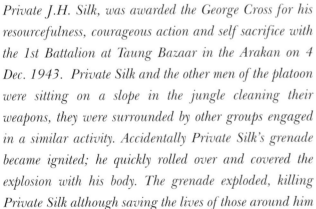

Private J.H. Silk, was awarded the George Cross for his resourcefulness, courageous action and self sacrifice with the 1st Battalion at Taung Bazaar in the Arakan on 4 Dec. 1943. Private Silk and the other men of the platoon were sitting on a slope in the jungle cleaning their weapons, they were surrounded by other groups engaged in a similar activity. Accidentally Private Silk's grenade became ignited; he quickly rolled over and covered the explosion with his body. The grenade exploded, killing Private Silk although saving the lives of those around him

Captain Simon Latutin was awarded the George Cross for action taken on 29 December 1944. At a training school store at Somalie Gendarmerie, Mogadishu some Italian rockets and explosives were being taken out to take to another unit for their New Year's entertainment. Captain Latutin, along with another officer, a company sergeant major and a personal boy, were in this store selecting the explosives. For some reason a fire broke out inside the store, which set off a number of rockets, the store became a dangerous inferno. Captain Latutin, regardless of the danger to himself, plunged into the store and dragged out the officer, who was already seriously burnt. Although he was, by this time, himself alight, Latutin again headed back into the store and rescued the company sergeant major. Captain Latutin died the following day as a result of his injuries

A patrol led by Sergeant Garratt on the Austrian Yugoslav frontier

A patrol checking the identities of two civilian women, Austria c.1947. The 2nd Battalion was transferred from Greece to Austria in early 1947 for further peace-keeping duties

≈ CHAPTER 9 ≈

COLD WAR CONFRONTATIONS AND THE END OF EMPIRE
1947–1955

The world that emerged from the Second World War was very different. With India the leading voice, the British colonies began to call for independence; many passed off easily whilst for others the transition was less smooth. Added to this was the political climate of the era. The world had been split in two by the Iron Curtain and the West feared the spread of Communism, especially in Asia where it was thought countries would fall like dominoes into the Communist net, a fear only inflated by the Korean War from 1950 to 1953 and the anti-French Indo-China War occuring at the same period.

With the outbreak of the Second World War it was the turn of the 1st Battalion to be stationed in India. Just like the 2nd in the earlier war, most of the time there was spent moving from station to station, but this time it had to keep an eye on the frontiers for fear of a Japanese invasion from 1941 onwards and the German threat in the Middle East. India's politicians felt that the country's manpower, resources and land bases were being used to fight a war which had little to do with India, was definitely not of her causing, and done without the say of her people. In addition, with the entry of Japan into the war in December 1941, with its promises of the Great East Asia Co-prosperity Sphere and independence for all nationals, nationalist feelings began to increase in India and sabotage and subversive activities increased. One such incident flared up in 1942; on 14 July the National Congress Working Committee published a resolution demanding the withdrawal of British rule from India and threatened a large-scale struggle. On 8 August the National Congress met in Bombay and confirmed the resolution passed by the Working Committee. A day later all the committee's members were arrested and riots immediately broke out in Bombay and Delhi, before spreading eastwards across central India. Police and troops were involved in subduing the riots, which were fortunately ill-coordinated and ill-timed.

INDIAN INDEPENDENCE, 1947

During the Second World War the British Government had been so hard pressed to defend its Empire, especially in the Far East, that it had enlisted the help of the Indian Army in combating the Axis powers; this, however, came at a price. India, in return for her help, had been promised independence from British rule. Although independence for India was neither straightforward nor easy, it was finally granted on 15 August 1947. The end of the war saw the 1st Battalion still in India, stationed at Peshawar in the North West under the command of Lieutenant Colonel C.S. Howard. Shortly after moving to Shargarh in the Central Provinces, a mutiny of Indian Signals occurred at Jubbalpore and the Battalion received immediate orders to move there. Although the mutineers were quite out of control they had no firearms and thus the Battalion could quite easily round them up; this incident was just one of many uprisings in support of independence. In April 1947 under the command of Major F.M. De Butts the Battalion moved to Bombay where the British and Indian authorities were negotiating the terms of independence.

It was a difficult time for the Battalion. There was always underlying civil unrest threatening to erupt at the slightest provocation; the defence cuts initiated by the British Government meant that soldiers were returning home after demobilisation, but no new recruits were filling the gaps and the British Army had to tread carefully so as not to incite or stir up anti-British feelings. On Independence Day, 2 August 1947, the 1st Battalion were the only British forces to participate in the parade with the Indian Army and on 28 February 1948 they were honoured to be the last British troops to march out of the jewel of the British Empire. Guards of Honour were provided by the Royal Indian Navy, the 3rd Indian Grenadiers, the 1st Mahratta Light Infantry, the 2nd Battalion the Royal Sikh Regiment and the 3rd/5th Royal Gurkha Rifles, for a moving ceremony. The 1st Battalion, under the command of Lieutenant Colonel J.R.I. Platt, together with the Regimental Colours, slow marched through the Gateway of India in Bombay to the awaiting troop-ships. On return to England it amalgamated with the 2nd Battalion in June 1948 and soon after this new Battalion took over the duties of the Light Infantry Brigade Training Centre, at Bordon in Hampshire.

India's independence marked the end of an era and of a link between the Regiment and the Indian continent that lasted for 126 years. The Regiment has, however, left its mark on the country, including many

The Colour Party leaving Bombay Harbour, February 1948

The Colour Party marching through the Gateway to India, February 1948

graves and memorials to the soldiers who died whilst serving there, and reminders such as the Regimental Badge carved into the hills above Cherat. The Regiment had done much to protect its border, not only in major wars such as those with Afghanistan, Burma and the two world wars, but also in localised tussles such as the Mohmand Expedition; it had also helped to ease the process of independence, long promised and finally delivered. It is fair to say that throughout its history and from all the countries and continents with which the Regiment gained links, those forged with India were probably the strongest and most valued.

The Malayan Emergency, 1952–1955

The Malayan Emergency, which broke out in 1948 and lasted for the next twelve years, saw the British embroiled in one of many struggles to achieve colonial independence but which also became a fight against Communist insurgency.

The Malayan Emergency, so called as the term 'war' was likely to cause unnecessary harm to the economy, was fought between the Malayan Communist Party (MCP) on the one side and the British and Malayan authorities on the other. Malaya had had a Communist Party since 1925 and it was from this party that the MCP emerged at the end of the Second World War and immediately began calling for independence for Malaya from its colonial masters. The MCP consisted mainly of Chinese, and indeed the Chinese sent many Communist agents to that country. Although the Communist party was illegal it grew in popularity until destroyed by the British authorities for its attempts to install a Communist government during the 1930s. During the Second World War Britain armed and supported the MCP as, after the fall of Singapore, it provided the only organised resistance against Japan; however, this provided invaluable training for the MCP in guerrilla tactics and also the admiration of the Malayan people. Soon after the war, during the campaign against the proposals for the Federation of Malaya in 1947, the MCP turned against the British. To the MCP, the British agreement to the Federation of Malaya signalled that they wanted to control the independence process in order to stop the development of a Communist government in Malaya. In addition, the new leader of the MCP, Chin Peng, believed that an armed revolt would ensure a Communist government. These two factors meant an insurrection against the British was inevitable.

In June 1948 the uprising began with the murder of three British rubber planters. This marked the beginning of a continuous terror campaign by the Communists, known as the CTs (CTs was the abbreviation for Communist not Chinese Terrorists – the Malayan Communist Party's armed force was titled 'The Malayan Races Liberation Army, [MRLA] and included Malays and Tamils, originally plantation workers from Southern India, but they seldom totalled even 10% of the MRLA) by the British, which saw the murdering, butchering, torturing and terrorising of the British and native inhabitants. They also sabotaged the infrastructure by destroying train lines and generating civil unrest. This soon evolved into attacks upon the British and Malayan security forces, usually in the form of ambushes and guerrilla attacks. The CT force numbering around 10000, was mainly jungle based with a vast support network of Chinese living in towns and villages who, often from fear of reprisals, supported the CTs. The first attacks took the British by surprise. After initial successes against formed bodies of CTs the Army was forced into a holding operation. This was necessary because of its lack of experience against the now smaller, more elusive bands of CTs and because of the large number of inexperienced National Servicemen serving in operational units. The next step the British Army took was to rehouse 600,000 squatters living in villages on the fringes of the jungle, used by the CTs as refuge and as a source of information and food. The squatters were moved to 'New Villages' where they could be isolated from the guerrillas, cutting off the rebels' food supply and where strict curfews could be applied. They also set up a reward system whereby anyone offering information on the CTs received a cash bonus: this led to many informing on their comrades.

It was into this situation that the 1st Battalion arrived in November 1952. Its first task was to undergo intensive jungle training at the Jungle Warfare School at Kota Tinggi in Johore. This training was important and was undergone by all new regiments entering Malaya. The weapons used in the jungle differed from those used in Europe and the term 'Shoot to Kill' had to be learned. Each soldier had to learn how to live in the jungle, how to lay an ambush and how to find his way around jungle terrain. Sergeant David Cridge of 'B' Company of the 1st Battalion explains his experiences at Johore:

A large camp-site had been constructed just across the causeway from Singapore, in the state of Johore. There the lads would over the next six weeks become acclimatised to tropical conditions whilst learning a few basic skills. Such as, if you take off a warm canvas jungle boot and drop it carelessly at the side of the bed, during the night some insect will make it home, and if that insect is a scorpion your yell of pain will awaken the whole camp-site. But it wasn't that: death struck twice at that camp, and suddenly the Malayan Emergency became reality.

The arrival of the 1st Battalion in Singapore, November 1952

A visit by Anthony Head, Secretary of State for War, to 'D' company of the 1st Battalion, 1952

The first involved some young lad getting the feeling of a Sten gun, a cheap and nasty light automatic brought out during the Second World War by the British to use German 9 millimetre captured ammunition. The exact details are somewhat vague, but I knew the weapon was extremely unreliable and a jolt would often cause it to fire. Unfortunately in this case we had our first fatality. A few days later we had a grandstand view of low-level bombing.

Hundreds watched a twin engine RAF plane swoop in and drop bombs from about 500 feet into the jungle. A blast from one of the bombs visibly rocked the aircraft, it almost immediately upended and plunged into the dense jungle, within half a mile of where we stood.

In January 1953 tactical advance parties left the training camp and the rest of the battalion soon followed to its new camp at Selangor. The first operation carried out by the Somersets was an extension of that being carried out by the Suffolk Regiment whom the 1st Battalion had relieved. It was a successful campaign that saw the men in an area of jungle swamp south-west of Kuala Lumpur trying to capture the CT commander Liew Siew Fook. With the support of harassing fire from the Royal Navy, Liew Siew Fook soon surrendered and wasted no time in leading the Battalion straight to Lau Cheng, the chief CT in South Selangor, who was killed on 2 March 1953. In just five months, the Battalion had helped to clear the North Swamp of terrorists.

Life in the area was not easy for the soldiers as Corporal Welch describes in his memoirs:

My first trip into the swamp was a bit different, from solid ground to ankle deep to waist deep ... Visibility was around twenty yards if you were lucky. But hard going as it felt like your feet were in six inches of soft mud and roots. The water the colour of cold tea without milk, and leaches galore, and mosquitoes as big as blackbirds ... living in a tent with thunder boxes and lots of flies and a rodent burrow not too far away and no showers as we relied on the sea ... I realised the sea was good for some things but not for others and was not a complete cleanser. It might have got the top dirt off but little more and we had run out of salt water soap. So the inevitable happened, jungle sores were rife. We had been spending the odd night or two in derelict squatters huts ... and I think we got body lice from there, and we got lousy in big way ... We had an FFI (free from infection) it was my first since training and all of a sudden the Army got its act together. The entire platoon was lined up out in the rubber with both jungle uniforms and jungle boots. We were told to strip and the Medical Officer inspected each man ... Then all uniforms, towels and jungle-boots, in fact anything worn

Number 5 platoon whilst on jungle operations

An abandoned bandit basha

*in the swamp went into a heap and petrol poured over them and burnt …
We had lice patrols and inspections carried out by us NCOs and two weeks
later another FFI and all of a sudden we were eligible for six jabs per man.
The headquarters medic not our own, licking his lips pushing in the needle,
some other medic followed with a syringe with a mix of three vaccines, and
injected each man and removing the syringe. The needle stayed put and
another medic with another syringe with a three mix did the same. Six mixes
per man all down one needle and the last one pulled it out, and deposited
the needle in meths to sterilise it. One needle went through the whole
platoon and for my money I thought the needles were far from sharp in fact
they felt like the old man's garden fork!*

Above left: *A group of terrorists being
led out of the jungle*

Above: *A mortar firing at night*

Although the campaign in Malaya started off well with the Battalion
seeing immediate action, for most of the time patrols often led to
nothing, with companies spending days patrolling in the jungle search-
ing for an elusive enemy, whilst being constantly attacked by insects and
animals. After the successful conclusion of activities in the North
Swamp, attention was turned to the hills that lay to the east of Kuala
Lumpur where Yong Kwo, a second-ranking CT was based. In
September 1953, a full-scale operation was launched against Yong Kwo,
which aimed to cut off food supplies entering the jungle. Several
surrenders followed between autumn 1953 and June 1954. In August
1954 the Battalion was taken off operational duties for two months in
order to retrain. Upon returning to jungle operations in October 1954,
it became responsible for the State of Selangor. In December it moved
again, to the State of Pahang.

A visit to Malaya by the American Vice President, Richard Nixon

It was whilst based in Pahang that the Battalion pulled off its greatest achievement of the Malayan Campaign. On 23 January 1955 Major Haigh and his batman Private F.G. Davis, were carrying out a follow-up operation. On the fourth day of the operation the group were fired on but after a tense ten-minute battle the terrorists fled. From the dead and wounded it was discovered that they had surprised an important meeting of the area's CTs, amounting to more than 30 terrorists. For their actions Major Haigh has awarded the MC and Private Davis, who saved Major Haigh's life, the MM. The remainder of the campaign in Pahang was equally successful, with the Battalion managing to reduce the terrorist group in that area to just six leaderless men.

On 9 September 1955 a major change occurred in the attitude to the terrorists; the Malayan government declared an amnesty, which meant that captures and surrenders became more important than kills. It was soon after this amnesty that the 1st Battalion was relieved by the Royal Lincolnshire Regiment. Its tour in Malaya was a success by any standards. In total it killed 54 bandits and captured seven, as well as clearing the North Swamp, South Swamp and Pahang of terrorists.

On 31 August 1957 Britain granted independence to Malaya, and the reasons behind the armed insurrection disappeared. By 1960 the Malayan Emergency was all but over and the end was officially declared on 31 July 1960. The Somersets' three-year tour in the country helped considerably to bring a successful conclusion to the war and a reasonably peaceful transfer to independence. Throughout the tour the

Above: *General Templer, Lieutenant Colonel Brind and Major de Butts watching a machine gun in action*

Left: *Number 10 platoon in bivouacs on the edge of a helicopter landing zone during operation 'BOOT', April 1953*

A jungle patrol by members of 'A' company

contribution made by the National Serviceman was considerable. On the Battalion's return to England in October 1955, it marched through Taunton, excercising its Freedom of the County Town.

The Suez Crisis followed in 1956 and the Battalion was mobilised and sent to Malta, but only the Anti-Tank Platoon as part of 40 Commando Royal Marines deployed to Suez. The remainder of the Battalion went to Cyprus to help counter the EOKA threat.

The Battalion returned to England in January 1957 and in 1958 became the Infantry's Demonstration Battalion at Warminster. It was at Knook Camp, Warminster in September 1959, before a large assembly of families and friends that the final parade of the 1st Battalion of The Somerset Light Infantry took place. Subsequently those selected for the new Regiment moved to Osnabruck for the amalgamation with The Duke of Cornwall: Light Infantry to become The Somerset and Cornwall Light Infantry. The new Regiment comprised one regular battalion stationed in Osnabruck and two Territorial Army battalions – 4th/5th Battalion The Somerset Light Infantry (TA) and the 4th/5th Battalion The Duke of Cornwall's Light Infantry (TA). The Regimental Depot was at Bodmin and the Regimental Headquarters at Mount Street, Taunton. The regular Battalion received new colours in May 1962 whilst stationed in Gibraltar, the colours being presented on behalf of The Queen by Field Marshal The Lord Harding of Petherton, The Somerset Light Infantry's most distinguished officer.

The Battalion subsequently served in West Berlin and Gravesend and carried out an operational tour in Aden before being amalgamated with the other county Light Infantry Regiments in 1968, to become The Light Infantry.

The Somerset and Cornwall Light Infantry receiving new colours, Gibraltar, 1962

Chapter 10

Somerset's Militia
and Territorial Forces

England has had a local militia force since the Middle Ages: a trained
local part-time force used for local and home defence in times of invasion or rebellion. The Militia Act of 1757 established one or more militia
regiments per county, which were raised from volunteers and conscripts
chosen by ballot from each parish. Until 1871 the raising and training of
the local militia, and appointment of officers, was the responsibility of the
Lord Lieutenant of the county. During peacetime the militia would meet
for annual training and drill, in preparation for more turbulent times. In
periods of unrest, once the militia regiments had been mobilised, they fell
under the control of the commander-in-chief of the Army and could be
sent anywhere in the British Isles, though not overseas.

During the late eighteenth and nineteenth centuries other territorial
forces were formed; the Yeomanry, which was a cavalry corps; the
Volunteers, raised by private or municipal enterprise for local defence;
and the local militia. The Volunteers were dissolved in 1813 and the
local militia in 1816, but the Yeomanry continued, acting mainly as an
armed police force, until 1859 when its number was dramatically
reduced. In 1859, with fears of foreign invasion, volunteer forces were
again formed, although they had little connection with the War Office,
until 1873, when a small number of soldiers formed a permanent staff
for each county regiment.

With the reorganisation of the army system in 1881 the county militia
regiments became the 3rd battalions and the Volunteers became the 4th
battalions and sometimes the 5th, depending on their numbers. 1908
saw the renaming of the Militia as the Special Reserve; the Volunteers
and the Yeomanry were renamed the Territorial Forces. Territorial
Forces were only to serve at home, although members could volunteer
for service overseas. Those in the Special Reserve held the same position as normal army reservists, who could be called up in times of war.
In 1924 the Special Reserve was again renamed, as the Supplementary

Reserve. It was not disbanded until 1953. In 1940 the Local Defence Volunteers, renamed the Home Guard, were formed for home defence, and this body lasted in different reincarnations until 1957.

THE MILITIA

The Somerset Militia dates back to 1559 when a body of men was raised to guard the county, comprising 1000 men and officers. In 1588 came mobilisation of men to resist the Armada, with 4000 being raised in the county. Throughout the seventeenth century the Somerset Militia continued to exist, although spasmodically, and it is not until 1757 that we see a regular force forming. Under the provisions of the 1757 Act, Somerset had to provide 840 men, and the necessary steps for meeting this quota began in 1758 with three-fifths of the number being recruited by January 1759. In June 1762 the Somerset Militia were detailed with the guarding of French prisoners of war at Exeter. In 1763, at the end of the Seven Years War, the 2nd Battalion of the Somerset Militia was disbanded and the 1st increased in size. Training of the Militia then became a regular occurrence, with the companies coming together for twenty-eight days' training and exercises each year.

Camp of the 1st Division of the Somerset militia, autumn manoeuvres, Yannaton Down, Dartmoor, 1873

Between 1763 and 1881 the Somerset Militia were employed in activities such as putting down local riots, ensuring the peace, escorting and guarding prisoners, suppressing smuggling and guarding fire beacons. During this period militia soldiers often joined the regular forces, especially in times of conflict such as the Crimean War. As mentioned, 1881 saw the introduction of the Territorial Act and the 1st and 2nd Somerset Militia became the 3rd and 4th Battalions The Somerset Light Infantry. Then in 1900 followed an embodiment of the Militia in response to the Boer War. By 1908 the provisions of the 1907 Territorial and Reserve

Forces Act were in force and the Militia ceased to exist. Militia battalions were either disbanded or changed into reserve battalions.

The 1st Militia kitchens and staff, Leigh camp, Blagdon, Somerset, 1877

THE TERRITORIAL FORCES

The life of the Somerset Volunteer forces began on 29 March 1794 when the Grand Jury assembled at Taunton to consider certain plans for the defence of the kingdom. They resolved unanimously that they should be ready at all times to be able to protect the kingdom, and the sheriff was detailed to call a meeting to consider what would be the best way of doing so. The officers of the Taunton Loyal Volunteers were appointed on 21 June 1794. April saw a meeting to establish a regiment of Light Cavalry, which became known as the Somerset Fencible Cavalry. On 5 May 1794 a list of the gentlemen and yeomen who were willing to serve in a Yeomanry troop was produced. By the end of May 1795 there were volunteer troops in Bath and Taunton, along with the Loyal Somerset Regiment of Fencible Infantry, troops of Yeomanry at Castle Cary, Taunton, North Perrott, Yeovil, Brymore, Milverton, Frome and Martock, and companies of infantry at Taunton, Somerton, Bridgwater, Langport, Frome and Wells. However, there seems to have been no centralised control and the administration was confused.

With the signing of the Treaty of Amiens with France in 1801, moves were made to disband the volunteer forces, as it was believed England was now safe from invasion. But the Government did not want to disband all the Yeomanry troops and so those that wanted to remain were allowed to do so. The West Somerset Yeomanry agreed to the terms of service during peacetime along with the East Somerset Yeomanry. With the threat of war with France looming again in 1803, volunteer units were again formed; in Somerset it is estimated that 20,000 men came forward for service. At this time, to join the Yeomanry, a man had to provide his own horse, arms, clothing and equipment. After the Battle of Trafalgar in 1805 the Volunteer Force was again reduced in size and by 1813, the only territorial units left in Somerset were the East and West Regiments of Yeomanry, the Frome and East Mendip Volunteer Cavalry (which in 1814 changed its title to the North Somerset Yeomanry) and a company of the Bath Volunteer Regiment.

The Volunteer Forces remained low in numbers until 1859 when relations with France again became strained. The home defence forces were again increased with Rifle Volunteer Corps being raised in Taunton and Bath, and sub-units in places such as Williton, Yeovil and Glastonbury. In total 28 independent Rifle Corps were formed in the county, which were organised into three Somersetshire Rifle Volunteer Corps. With the army reorganisation in 1881 the Corps were consolidated into battalions, taking the titles, 1st, 2nd and 3rd Volunteer Battalions (Prince Albert's) Somerset Light Infantry. At first, Rifle Volunteers had to clothe and equip themselves, so it was often members of the richer classes who joined; however, in 1863, the Volunteer Act granted 30 shillings per annum for every Volunteer and poorer members began to join.

The South Petherton Rifle Volunteers, c.1860

A militia cycle platoon from the 2nd Volunteer Battalion, 1896

The officers of the 2nd Volunteer Battalion, Minehead, 24 July 1896

With the declaration of war against the Boers in October 1899, there was no immediate panic, and it was thought a large militia and volunteer force would not be needed. However, with the first defeats of the British Army, offers of support came flooding in. The Yeomanry and Volunteer Forces were often the first to offer help; the North and West Somerset Yeomanry both contributed a company to the Regiments of Imperial Yeomanry that were raised. A Volunteer Active Service Company was also formed from men of the three Somerset Volunteer Battalions; this company was attached to the 2nd Battalion The Somerset Light Infantry for service in South Africa.

The West Somerset Yeomanry outside Clarke's Hotel, Taunton, 1900

The West Somerset Yeomanry horse lines, Dulverton camp, Somerset, 1909

The South Africa war had shown up the cracks in the British military system and the Secretary of State for War, Viscount Haldane, initiated a thorough reorganisation of the British Army. The most important aspect of this reorganisation was the reconstituting of the Militia, Yeomanry and Volunteer Forces as the Territorial Force. The Territorial and Reserve Force Act of 1907 disbanded 23 militia units, whilst the remainder were transferred to the Special Reserves, a new force, which aimed to be the main Army Reserve. The Yeomanry and Volunteer Forces merged into the Territorial Force, which was to be the only British auxiliary force. The local impact of this legislation was that the three volunteer battalions became the 4th and 5th (Territorial Force) Battalions and the 3rd (Militia) Battalion became a Special

Reserve Unit. The 4th (Militia) Battalion was disbanded. The county was also required to keep two corps of cavalry and thus the North and West Somerset Yeomanry Corps remained.

With the outbreak of the Great War in 1914, the Territorial function of the county expanded. The 4th and 5th Battalions were subdivided into the 1/4th, 2/4th, 3/4th, 1/5th, 2/5th and 3/5th and saw action in India, Palestine, Burma, France, Belgium and Mesopotamia; other battalions remained at home, supplying drafts for the units fighting overseas. The North Somerset Yeomanry saw action in France and Flanders during the war, but the type of warfare employed meant that great cavalry charges were no longer possible. The West Somerset Yeomanry became the 12th Battalion of the Somerset Light Infantry and saw service at Gallipoli and in Palestine. The end of the war saw the disbandment of the additional regiments. The war had taught that an increasing reliance on artillery was needed and less dependence on cavalry. Thus, the War Office decided that the West Somerset Yeomanry should be converted into a Field Artillery Brigade.

A demonstration tank with the North Somerset Yeomanry, c.1928

With the outbreak of the Second World War the Territorial element of the Regiment was again expanded. The 4th Battalion helped to form the 6th Battalion, whilst the 5th helped form the 7th. Again, the county formed volunteer battalions, in the form of the Home Guard, to help defend the county from attack. Between 1944 and 1946, the territorial battalions were either disbanded or put into suspended animation, but in April 1947 the 4th was reformed a territorial unit. In 1954, the Battalion's title was changed to the 4/5th Battalion, and then in 1959 with the amalgamation of The Somerset Light Infantry and The Duke of Cornwall's Light Infantry, the Battalion became The Somerset Light Infantry (Prince Albert's) (TA), with its headquarters at Taunton. In 1967, the Territorial Battalion was amalgamated with the County Yeomanry Regiments to form the Somerset Yeomanry and Light Infantry, but before this unit could be fully established it was reduced in 1969 to a small cadre. In 1971 came a nationwide expansion of the Territorial Army and the Battalion was re-formed as the 6th (Somerset and Cornwall) Battalion The Light Infantry (Volunteers). In 1999 this was disbanded, leaving 'B' (Somerset Light Infantry) Company The Rifle Volunteers as the only surviving Somerset Infantry Territorial Unit.

A soldier learning to shoot at the Light Infantry Training Centre, Bordon, Hampshire c.1950s

Somerset has an even longer link with militia forces than it does with a regular standing army. Although the territorial and militia battalions do not hold swathes of battle honours, they were ready to defend the county and country when needed and even helped to contribute to British victories overseas in the wars of the early twentieth century.

Her Royal Highness Princess Margaret inspecting a 4th Battalion Guard of Honour, Bath, 1 May 1948

CONCLUSION

On 10 July 1968 the curtain fell on The Somerset Light Infantry, its brief life as The Somerset and Cornwall Light Infantry having been ended with yet more Army reform. During its history spanning almost 300 years the Regiment had distinguished itself time and again and helped bring glory to both its home county and its kingdom. It had received a vote of thanks in Parliament and had a future king, King George VI, as its Colonel-in-Chief. It was truly an 'Illustrious Garrison'.

The spirit of the Regiment lives on today in The Light Infantry, its badge containing the bugle which was common to its former regiments; the county town of Somerset still bears the familiar names of the Regiment, such as Jellalabad, and in churches all over the county memorials stand to those who fought and fell with the Regiment. More important still, old soldiers live on to continue the memory of the inspiring acts their predecessors performed.

The Regimental Band and Bugles marching through Bournemouth on a Territorial Army recruiting march, c.1950s

A 4th Battalion Colour Party, c.1950s